MY SHELTER

By Marti Owens

Copyright © 2015 by Marti Owens

My Shelter
by Marti Owens

Printed in the United States of America.

ISBN 9781498445115

All rights reserved solely by the author. The author guarantees all contents are original and do not infringe upon the legal rights of any other person or work. No part of this book may be reproduced in any form without the permission of the author. The views expressed in this book are not necessarily those of the publisher.

Unless otherwise indicated, Scripture quotations are taken from the King James Version (KJV) – public domain

www.xulonpress.com

Introduction

This past summer I was led to research and post some scriptures and my understanding of them on the social media website Facebook. It soon became something that I looked forward too. It encouraged me to look deeper into God's word. It challenged me to find verses that really meant something special to me and to try to explain why they did. As I continued this endeavor I started having responses from my friends about how much they appreciated the verses. The feedback I received was overwhelming and humbling to me. Many would say that a particular verse was just what they needed to hear that day. A lifelong girlfriend was at my house one day and we were reading over some of the devotions I had written. She suggested I write a book. Of course, she's my friend so I expected her to believe in me and what I felt like God was leading me to do. However, her words echoed back to me again and again. I knew that God had been working with me for a while, sending me scriptures or thoughts to look up in His word. At some point in August of this year I started writing devotions. I felt obedient in what I was doing and felt God pulling at me to keep it up. Here it is December and I've just made a HUGE leap of faith and signed with a publisher! I know that I've got a long way to go and I honestly have to say I'm scared to death. I know though that I'm willing to follow this through for my Lord. From the very beginning I knew the name of this book would be "My Shelter." I hope that somewhere in the words on these pages you will find hope, peace, love, courage and shelter in the true sense of the word. He truly is My Shelter.

In His service,
Marti Owens

DEDICATION

In loving memory of Betty Ruth Love Buckner
and Milton Elgin (Buck) Buckner

Table of Contents

Introduction v
Dedication vii
Acknowledgements xiii

Protection	15	Fruit of the Spirit	44
Misery	16	Worship	45
Home	17	Working	46
Hope	18	Weak	47
Trust	19	Intervention	48
Safe	20	Pure	49
Faith	21	Complete	50
Gift	22	Words of Anger	51
Peace	23	Shield	52
Prayer	24	Healed	53
Boldness	25	Emptiness	54
Promise	26	Giving	55
Humble	27	Fear	56
Teach	28	Rock	57
Needs	29	Respect	58
Comfort	30	Help	59
Praise	31	Train	60
Victory	32	Light	61
Grace	33	Thirst	62
Sing	34	Golden Rule	63
Preach	35	Witness	64
Confusion	36	Forgive	65
Amazed	37	Humble	66
Strength	38	Supplication	67
Sin	39	Growth	68
Love	40	Unity	69
Miracle	41	Church	70
Assurance	42	Sailing	71
Foundation	43	Friends	72

Calvary	73	Near	112
Guide	74	Banner	113
Decisions	75	Security	114
Idols	76	Defeated	115
Sacrifice	77	Speaking	116
Compassion	78	The Cross	117
Struggles	79	Agape	118
Joy	80	Angels	119
Time	81	Holy	120
Steadfastness	82	Forgiveness	121
Beloved	83	Thankful	122
Supply	84	Bought	123
Anxiety	85	Long Suffering	124
Hearing	86	Newness	125
Control	87	In The Beginning	126
Afraid	88	Confession	127
Choose	89	Power	128
Words	90	Eternity	129
Action	91	Lifted Up	130
Sheep	92	Chosen	131
Brokenhearted	93	Missing the Mark	132
Burdens	94	Prepared	133
Distress	95	Bucket List	134
Filled with Joy	96	Disconnected	135
Deliverance	97	Separated	136
Tranquility	98	Magnified	137
Given	99	Comfort	138
New Creation	100	Exercise	139
Doubt	101	Final Words	140
Worry	102	Amazement	141
Creator	103	A Worthy Walk	142
Promises	104	Beauty	143
Sleep	105	A Father's Love	144
Rescued	106	Patience	145
Control	107	Hero's	146
Sharing	108	Restoration	147
Provision	109	Called	148
Bigger	110	Relinquished	149
Sufficient	111	Secured	150

Weary 151	Divine Intervention 174
Formed 152	Multi Task 175
Parched 153	Give It Up 176
Riches 154	Speak Up. 177
The Word. 155	Reach Out 178
Shine 156	Sight Restored. 179
Stop, Look and Listen. 157	Rest 180
The Lamb 158	Renewal. 181
Judging 159	Shelter. 182
The Great Commission 160	He Holds Us 183
WWJD. 161	Gossip 184
Hunger. 162	Master 185
Direction 163	Hurting 186
Confidence 164	Know Peace 187
Listening 165	Crying 188
Serenade 166	Serve 189
Calm 167	Unsinkable 190
Courage. 168	Willing 191
Honor 169	Gratitude 192
Supplier. 170	Heritage. 193
Claim It 171	Shine 194
Whole 172	Relief. 195
Safe 173	Immersed. 196

About the Author 197
Work Cited. 199

ACKNOWLEDGEMENTS

I want to thank my Abba Daddy God for giving me the words that are on these pages. There are so many people that walked with me on this journey I could never name them all. With that being said I want to thank my immediate family for listening over and over to the rough drafts and to my friends that encouraged me to write to begin with. A huge thank you goes out to all who proofread my manuscript, worked on the cover design and worked with me on the submission process. To all of the prayer warriors that prayed me through the days when I wasn't sure I would continue, thank you!

Philippians 1:3

I thank my God upon every remembrance of you.

Protection

Psalm 36: 7

How excellent is thy lovingkindness, O God! Therefore the children of men put their trust under the shadow of thy wings.

I was raised on a farm. My parents and grandparents had cows, hogs, goats, chickens and a lot of other farm animals. Many times growing up I watched a hen hatch a new batch of eggs and mother her little chicks. She was always protective of those little furry creatures. She would watch to make sure that they were following her when she moved, she would check around her to make sure there was nothing there to harm them. That mother hen would flap her wings and gather her chicks under them if it rained or was cold. In other words, she provided them shelter. This verse tells us that God provides shelter for His children. Can you imagine Him just reaching down with His arms and gathering you up and just hovering over you? I can! How many times have you felt His comfort or peace like wings covering you? This is our great big God leaning down and wrapping us in His arms, extending His spiritual wings to cover us in our time of need. Will you trust God to shelter you each day?

God help us to always seek shelter in Your arms. Help us to put our whole faith in Your love knowing that You will shelter us with Your wings.

Misery

Job 3: 20

Wherefore is light given to him that is in misery, and life unto the bitter in soul.

How many times have you heard someone say "I'm miserable?" I have heard it many times referring to many different situations. We may say we're miserable because we ate too much, or maybe we worked too hard, or due to the burdens of life being so heavy. Misery from overeating or over work goes away on its own. Misery, the deep down in your heart and soul misery doesn't normally just go away. I believe that in this world today there are so many miserable people. I believe they are looking for answers, many of them in the wrong places with the wrong people. God's word tells us that light will be given to us in our misery. That light comes from God. He sent his son Jesus to light the world with a light that will shine eternally. The light which gives us light and peace down deep in our souls. When you find yourself in despair and are feeling miserable, look toward the light! The light of our Savior!

Thank You God so much for giving us light that will flood out our misery. Thank You that we can come to You and find solace for our broken hearts.

HOME

II Corinthians 5: 1

For we know if our earthly house of this tabernacle were dissolved, we have a building of God, an house not made with hands, eternal in the Heavens.

We may save for years in order to buy or build a home. We may conjure up pictures of our dream home in our minds, and make files with pictures we like. We may go see other homes that look like we want our home to look. In other words, we spend a lot of time and money preparing our home for earthy living. Now, here is the best news ever about homes! We have a heavenly home! Yes, that's right. One that we won't have to toil for or plan for or dream about. It's here for the taking. We only have to believe that Jesus Christ died for us! He has promised us a home that will never lose its value, never need repairs and will stand firm for all eternity!

Father, thank You for my heavenly home that I will live in one day because You bought it just for me.

HOPE

John 14:2, 3

In my Father's house are many mansions: if it were not so, I would have told you. I go to prepare a place for you. And if I go and prepare a place for you, I will come again, and receive you unto myself; that where I am, there ye may be also.

Recently, a friend and I had the honor of sharing a little bit about this scripture to a child where I work. His dad had recently passed away and he became upset during the day. My friend was holding back tears as she tried to think of ways to let this child know that his dad was happy in Heaven. She threw out a question at me. "What's the first thing you get when you get to Heaven?" Since I hadn't been in on any of the conversation until that point, I said "A crown!" Then she asked what else and my second answer was, "A mansion!" The little boy's face changed right then. We ask the child to describe what he thought his dad's mansion looked like. The conversation went on for a while as the boy thought about things his dad may have in his mansion. Later, as he was feeling better he remarked, "I didn't know you got a crown too" God used me and my friend that day to reassure this little boy that God does have a mansion waiting for us in heaven. He used us to give hope by using this scripture to give peace in that little boy's heart. I'm so thankful that my friend knew where to lead this child for answers.

God, thank You for hiding Your word in our hearts so that when we need to use it to uplift or comfort another that we will have it. Thank You for allowing a little boy a glimpse of hope from Your word.

Trust

Isaiah 57:2

He shall enter into peace: they shall rest in their beds, [each one] walking [in] his uprightness.

When I think of peace I tend to think of world peace. However, I believe that God is talking about personal peace in this scripture. I believe He wants to assure us that if we place our trust in Him we can and will have this peace. It may not mean that the problems we are encountering go away, but it means we will have inner peace regardless of what is going on. We will be able to lie down at night, close our eyes and rest because we have given the fight to God.

Lord, I pray that You will remind us of how much You love us and how You want what is best for us at all times. Help us to trust You with everything in our lives, big and small and lay us down in perfect sleep knowing that You are in control.

SAFE

Proverbs 3: 25-26

Be not afraid of sudden fear, either of the desolation of the wicked, when it cometh. For the Lord shall be thy confidence, and shall keep thy foot from being taken.

If you turn on the television at all today, you will find so much evil being reported. You will find many things occurring in our world that are scary. Right now we are facing terrorist among us, hatred of each other, and hatred for our beliefs. We hear stories of Christians being beheaded for believing in God. We find disease of all kinds infiltrating our lives. We are becoming fearful of so many of these things. We know when we read God's word that these things are going to happen. We know they are signs God told us would come to pass before His glorious returning. God gave us this scripture as a reminder that we don't have to be afraid, we are His children and He will take care of us. The verse says do not be afraid of the desolation of the wicked when it comes. Not if it comes but when. God knew these days were coming for us. He knew we would need to be reassured of His steadfast love. This verse tells us that He is our confidence and that He will keep us from being taken. We are his children! We are safe in his love! Eternally! There are things this world can throw at us and there are things people can do to us. Those things are external. Do not fear for our souls and hearts belong to our Creator! He will see us through all of these present evils and we will be victorious because He lives in us!

Father, help us not to fear because nothing in this world is greater than You and Your love. Help us as we continue on this journey.

FAITH

Hebrews 11:1

Now faith is the substance of things hoped for, the evidence of things not seen.

This week I have had an onslaught of the devils work. He's been snapping at my feet every which way! I have prayed and prayed about the outcome of these things. I have begged God as humbly as I know how to fix these problems, to take charge of the situation. Now it's left up to me to have the faith to leave it with Him. That's where the rubber meets the road, so to speak. It's not difficult when you are a believer to cry to your heavenly Father for your needs. It's not hard to fall on your face and beg for mercy. The hard thing is to have the continued faith that God knows our needs. To believe that He knew before any of this happened exactly how it was going to play out. We have to grab hold of our faith and pour out our hearts to God, if you've already done that then the next step is to leave the problems with the Father! He knows what's best! Surprisingly enough it may not be what or how we are praying for the problem to be resolved. There again is where our faith must be strong and complete in Christ. We must know that God is in control and that he has the right answers.

Lord, today my heart is heavy with needs for my family members, yet I am so blessed. I'm blessed to be able to come before You and give You my problems. I'm blessed to be assured that You are in control and that You have the right answers. Thank You God for listening to my woes and for being faithful.

GIFT

Luke 2:11

For unto you is born this day in the city of David a Saviour, which is Christ the Lord.

I know as Christians some holidays we observe mean more to us than others. I have always loved Christmas. I love giving gifts. I had rather watch a friend or loved one open a gift than get one any day. So when I go back especially at Christmas time and read this passage I am overwhelmed with love and joy. I can't image what it must have been like for God, the Creator of Heaven and earth to send His only son to us as a babe in a manger. He knew before He sent Jesus what purpose Jesus would have in the lives of men. He sent us a Redeemer! He not only sent us a babe in a manger that the shepherds worshipped, He sent us a man made of flesh. A man that was tempted by the devil himself and overcame that temptation. He was not just a man of flesh, but he was Emanuel! God with us! Of all of the names of God and there are many, Emanuel touches my heart the most. God planned for Jesus to live with us and in us and to be our guide. God planned for Jesus to be the King of King's and He meant for us to worship Him as such! I think about Christmas. I think about the real reason we celebrate with friends and family, and I am so thankful for the most precious gift I've ever been given. The gift of Jesus Christ. The gift of my Savior, my Redeemer, my Comforter, my Friend and my Abba Daddy God. Emanuel! God with us!

Father God, how can I ever thank You enough for Your son Jesus? I am so humbled by Your precious gift. Thank You God for giving the best You had.

PEACE

Psalm 119: 165

Great peace have they which love thy law, and nothing shall offend them.

Every verse I read this morning talked about peace. A peace that comes with loving God and doing His will. If we have God's peace then we won't need any other type of peace. His peace will be sufficient. When my mom was sick and dying, our pastor visited us in the hospital many times. On more than one occasion he told me he could see God's peace in me. Even though I was having to say an earthly goodbye to my best friend and my strongest cheerleader, I had peace. I suppose the reason I had this peace in the middle of heartbreak is because my God promised me He would give me peace. It's been seven years since the last time I saw my mom, seven years since I said that final goodbye, but God has been so faithful to continue to give me peace. You can have personal peace no matter what the external conditions are in your life. You can grab hold of God's promise in this verse and go forward in peace. He will sustain you each day, just like He promised.

Thank You Father for that peace that no one else can give. Thank You for holding me close when I needed You the most.

Prayer

Philippians 4:6

Be careful for nothing; but in every thing by prayer and supplication with thanksgiving let your requests be made known unto God.

I pray about everything! I really do! About a year ago my daughter's German shepherd, Sadie, didn't come home for dinner. My daughter was out of town and I called and told her that I knew something was wrong, because Sadie didn't come home. All through the night I stayed awake and waited for Sadie to show up. I got in my truck and drove the roads around our home looking for her but she wasn't anywhere close. My daughter came home early the next day and we looked for Sadie all day. We were heartbroken as we are big animal lovers. I couldn't eat or sleep, I was so worried, but I could and did pray. I cried out to God for the safe return of our furry friend. You see, I believe God created animals for us to enjoy. Since scripture tells us that He cares about the sparrows, I believed He cared what happened to Sadie. The whole weekend passed and even though we called local vet offices and posted pictures at stores and on social media websites she was still missing. That Sunday night I once again went before God and placed my petition for Sadie at His feet. I went to bed still praying in my heart for her return. Right before I went to sleep I heard my daughter and her husband go out again, I assumed to look for her. About ten minutes later, I received a phone call that Sadie had been found. Someone had seen a post and contacted them. She was perfectly fine and glad to be with her parents. Now, you may say this is ridiculous or that I shouldn't have bothered God about a dog, but I say that I serve such a great big God that hears all of my prayers and He sees our broken hearts, even when it's something like this. Don't miss out on God answering any of your prayers just because you didn't think it worthy to pray about.

Father, thank You for hearing our prayers even when they are about something simple. Thank You for Your protection over all of Your creation.

Boldness

Hebrews 4: 16

Let us therefore come boldly unto the throne of grace, that we may obtain mercy, and find grace to help in time of need.

Coming boldly before God is something a lot of us are probably skeptical about. We probably feel that we don't have the right to be bold with God. God wants us to bring our petitions to Him boldly. He wants us to come to Him just as we would to our parents, our spouses, or a trusted friend. Think about what happens when you have a problem. You go to someone that can give you advice. Someone you trust to lead you in the right way. When you go to them, you don't act shyly or backward about it, you go boldly. Why? Because you know they are there to help you. This is the manner that we should approach God with our longings. He waits on us to humble ourselves before Him, but that doesn't mean we can't be bold about our needs. Have you ever prayed for a friend's salvation? I bet you prayed with all of your heart, boldly asking God to save your friend. The same as when you are praying for healing for yourself or someone. You ask boldly. God extends His grace and His mercy and answers those prayers. There are so many ways to pray and so many ways for God to answer. Don't miss out on a blessing because you weren't bold enough to bring it to God.

Thank You God for allowing us to be bold when bringing our needs to You!

Promise

Jeremiah 32:27

Behold, I am the Lord, the God of all flesh, is there any thing too hard for Me?

I'm always amazed by this verse and how simple it is. I think we often forget how powerful, yet simple our God is. He just puts it out there for us. He doesn't make things difficult. That's where we come in. We have a hard time taking God at face value. Is there anything too hard for God? Not according to His word! We limit God! Sometimes, in my life, I find myself thinking that I'm not going to bother God with a particular need because it's too little. I can honestly say though that I've never thought a problem was too hard for God. Maybe it's just the amount of faith I have, maybe I realize there is no better place to take my problems. Who else do you know that has the power to turn your life around and make it different? Who else made a blind man to see, a leper clean or a dead man come to life? No, nothing is too hard for God. You don't believe me? Try Him! He won't let you down!

Father God, what assurance! How amazing are Your promises. Thank You for being bigger than all of my problems!

Humble

James 4:10

Humble yourselves in the sight of the Lord and he shall lift you up.

Are you humble? What a hard question for us to answer. I know that I need and want to be more humble. I think about how humble Jesus was during His walk on earth, He lived thirty three years on earth serving others, teaching others and showing us a spirit of meekness. It should have been difficult for Him to be humble; after all He was the Son of God! How many times have we met a person that was the child of someone important, only to watch them strut around showing off because of whom they are? They want the world's attention; they are saying "look at me!" Jesus said look! Look at my Father! Are you proud? Ouch! Do we go about bragging about what we have or what we've accomplished? Are you materialistic? Do you want to see how much stuff you can accumulate? As Christians, we are supposed to be pointing others to our Heavenly Father. As Christians, our pride should be in what our God is doing in our lives! We need to humble ourselves before God; the scripture gives us a promise, He will lift us up when we are humble before Him. Submit yourself to God because He is ready to do something good for you!

Lord, as we submit ourselves to You help us to remember who we need to be pointing people to.

TEACH

Deuteronomy 6:7

And thou shall teach them diligently unto thy children, and shall talk of them with thou sittest in thy house, and when thy walkest by the way, and when thou liest down, and when thou risest up.

It seems like from birth we are eager to make sure that our children are learning what they need to succeed in life. Nowadays, children begin preschool at a very early age. Time is spent teaching shapes and colors. We get so excited when they can recite their alphabet and count to ten. We need to be equally as excited to teach them God's word. We need to share what God is doing in our lives with our children. They should be able to see us living out God's word in our homes and lives. Do you say the blessing before meals with your family? Do you say your nighttime prayers? Do you give God glory and praise when a prayer is answered? Do you remember to teach your children about our Creator? God instructs us in His word to do just that. We need to walk the talk!

Thank You father for Your instructions for our families. Help us to remember how important it is for us to follow them.

NEEDS

Philippians 4:19

But my God shall supply all your need according to his riches in glory by Christ Jesus.

How awesome is this verse? Go back and read that first line again. My God shall supply ALL of your needs! I love that it covers all the bases. When we have more month than we do money, God will supply all of our needs. When our health is failing and we don't have answers, God will supply all of our needs. When we have to say earthly goodbyes to a loved one, God will supply all of our needs. I'm so thankful that just when I think I can't make it another day, God sends me just what I need to encourage me. Once, over 2000 years ago, the people needed a Savior to cover their sins. God supplied that need by sending Jesus. God is in the business of providing for His people.

God, I thank You for Your provisions. I thank You for Jesus and that through him You provided salvation for me from hell. I thank You that You provide for me on a daily basis.

Comfort

1 Thessalonians 5:11

Wherefore comfort yourselves together, and edify one another, even as also you do.

We know through the scriptures that God is our Divine Comforter, and that no one else gives the comfort that He gives. Many times in our lives we find that we need comfort not only from our Heavenly Father but also our friends and family. I think so many times we fail as humans to realize what a difference we can make in the lives of others. We callously go about our days while others all around us need a touch, a smile, a hug. We are God's feet and hands here on this earth. He equipped us with the ability to be sensitive to other's pain and needs. We have to be in tune to God in order to be in tune to other's needs.

God today we pray that You will give us a heart for others and that You show us those that we need to minister to for You.

Praise

1 Chronicles 16:25

For the Lord *is* great and greatly to be **praise**d; He *is* also to be feared above all **god**s.

When you look up the word praise in the dictionary this is what you find: "Praise –saying that a thing or person is good; words which tell the worth or value of a thing or person." Do you take the time to praise your Heavenly Father? Having been raised in church most of my life I was taught about an attitude of gratitude. Lifting up praises to God is one way to show that thankfulness. You can praise God in a lot of different ways. Taking a moment first thing in the morning to offer up your praise to Him is a great way to start the day. We have a minute of silence in the mornings where I work. I try to use this minuet just praising God and thanking Him for all He is in my life. What about lifting our hands to praise Him? Yes! I said lifting our hands! There are times in my life that I can't help but lift my hands up to Him. Sometimes, it's during my morning prayers and sometimes it's at church during the song service. The Lord deserves our praise and our recognition. We make time to praise all kinds of other things in our lives. Let's become more conscientious about praising our God!

Lord, we will praise Your Holy name! We will share Your word with others. Thank You for Your love.

VICTORY

II Corinthians 4:8

We are troubled on every side, yet not distressed; we are perplexed, but not in despair, persecuted, but not forsaken; cast down, but not destroyed.

What a relief to hear these words! Isn't it encouraging to know that no matter what might be thrown at you today you will be the victor? We face each day not knowing what it will hold. Depending on the circumstances right then in our lives, we may dread a new day or we may be waiting on it. This is the time to trust God and seek him to guide us through it. We may be facing health problems, marital problems, or problems with our kids. We may truly be perplexed at what is going on around us and wonder how on earth we are going to solve these issues. Our God is a God of peace and He does not want us to live in despair, no matter what may be going on. He has promised us that no matter what happens to us or around us we will not be crushed! This is because He cares for us and about what is happening in our lives every minute!

God thank You for the peace that is like no other peace! Thank You for showing us the way when we seek it from You.

GRACE

II Corinthians 12:9

And he said unto me, My grace is sufficient for thee: for my strength is made perfect in weakness. Most gladly therefore will I rather glory in my infirmities, that the power of Christ rest upon me.

How many people do you know battling cancer? I personally know far too many that are fighting it and having to endure all that comes with it. I watched my dad go through cancer twice and praise be to God, he beat it both times! I watched him go through treatments that made him sick and so weak. I saw him unable to eat and unable to stop being sick. It takes away so much of one's former self, although they fight diligently against it. I think about how hard my dad fought that disease. I think about all of those affected right now that are staying strong and pushing through all of the treatments they have to endure. I feel like this verse must have been written specifically for those fighting that horrible disease. I can't imagine how many times during the worst moments people call on God to help them, to ease the pain and sickness. How they must hear his gentle voice reassuring them that His grace is sufficient and that his strength is made perfect in their weakness. At this writing I know sweet saints that are finishing their journey here on earth, they are done with fighting this disease, but they are looking forward to seeing the God that sustained them though it all.

Thank You God in Heaven that Your grace is sufficient for me and for my family. Thank You that no matter what we face on this earth that You will sustain us.

SING

II Samuel 22:50

Therefore I will give thanks unto thee, O Lord, among the heathen, and sing praises unto thy name.

I love to sing! I don't have a beautiful voice, however, I just rejoined my church choir after years of pew sitting. I feel so much closer to God when I'm listening to or singing praise songs. I find that they say so much that my heart feels. I love to lift my hands to my Creator! I think about all of the ways that the Bible tells us that people praised God during biblical times. They sang, they played the tambourine, and they danced! Oh, yes they did! King David danced before the Lord! There are many ways to worship our Lord, so many ways to give thanks and praise to Him. We can give thanks and praise to Him by sharing His word with others, by lifting up His name in song, by lifting our hands up to Him. We can play a musical instrument for His glory and so much more. We all have gifts that He gave us. Are you using your gift to thank and praise Him today? It's not too late!

Lord, thank You so much for the beauty of music! Thank You that a song can touch my heart like nothing else.

Preach

II Timothy 4:2

Preach the word! Be ready in season *and* out of season. Convince, rebuke, exhort, with all **longsuffering** and teaching. to preach God's message. Do it willingly, even if it isn't the popular thing to do. You must correct people and point out their sins. But also cheer them up, and when you instruct them, always be patient.

You want me to preach? I don't have the words! There was another servant of God that didn't want to share God's word. He didn't feel like he had the words either, but as you know God enabled him to share anyway. God allowed his brother to be his speaker. Be ready! Do you think that Moses expected God to choose him to take the Israelites out of Egypt? Probably not. Moses wasn't even willing at first, because he felt inadequate. He didn't see himself as a preacher, because he wasn't a great speaker. How often do we use this as an excuse not to get up and do something for God? He may not be asking you to lead a nation out of their distress. He may only be asking you to lead a few kids in a Sunday school class or Wednesday night class. Maybe He just wants you to be ready and willing so that when the time comes, you will jump at the chance to serve Him, wherever it may be. God will use the most willing vessels in a mighty way!

Father, help me to be willing to share Your word anytime that You ask me to. Remind me that You will give me the words that You would have me speak.

Confusion

I Corinthians 14:23

For God is not the author of confusion but of peace, as in all the churches of the saints.

I'm continually shocked at how many things are happening all over the world that are confusing. I don't believe that God meant for our lives to be so mixed up. We see in God's word that He is not the author of all of this confusion around us. Why then do we seem to stay in a state of confusion? I believe it's because we take our focus off of God and we end up doubting things that we should know for certain. Maybe we doubt things like our faith or our relationship with Christ. I do believe that we sometimes doubt that God sees all and knows all. We wonder why things happen like they do. Why does a particular person get sick or die? Why do we end up jobless or feel we have no hope? We let the world confuse us, we look at what the world has to offer as opposed to what God has to offer. We have to claim His peace and remember that He is the Author of peace.

God I am so thankful that You are our answer for the confusing times that we live in. I'm so blessed to know that You knew about these times long ago and Lord, I'm so thankful that You are in control.

Amazed

I Samuel 12:24

Only fear the Lord, and serve Him in truth with all your heart; for consider what great things He has done for you.

Do you stand in awe of our Lord? We all should continually be amazed at all He has done for us! How many little things can you think of that you forget on a daily basis to be thankful for? A sunrise, a sunset, the love of a caring friend. How about that first breath you took this morning when you woke up? Yes, God has done so much more for us than even these things. If we thought about it, we could go on naming the great things. After you've named a few, take stock of what you are doing to thank Him. Are you serving Him? Serving Him by telling others about Him, reading and studying His word. This is more than just going to church on Sunday morning. Are you living for Him and being a witness for Him? Are you showing others the path to our King? Each new day is truly a gift for us to use as we see fit. Are we going to use it to serve the One that died for us?

Thank You God so much for all that You have done for me. I pray that I will spend my life serving You!

STRENGTH

II Samuel 22:23

God *is* my strength and power, And He makes my way perfect.

Some days I feel so frail and weak in my earthly body. I'm in good health but there are some days when I awake that I just feel tired. I imagine that you have days like this as well. I'm so thankful God is my strength and He will give me what I need to go through the day. Many times I've dropped to my knees to pray for God's strength, reminding myself that I am unable to make this journey without Him giving me the power to do so. It's reassuring to me when our bodies and minds become frail and begin to fail us that He is there beside us. It is Him who sustains our very life and we should take solace in knowing that He will never fail us in this area or any other as long as we seek Him. He will make our way perfect all the way to Heaven if we are His children.

God in heaven, thank You so much for being my power! How many times I've had to remind myself that You are in control of everything about my life. Thank You God for taking care of me.

Sin

Colossians 1:13

> Who hath delivered us from the power of darkness, and hath translated us into the kingdom of his dear Son:

I don't watch the news. It used to drive my mom crazy that I didn't know anything about current events. I had this habit of saying "If it didn't happen on my porch, I don't know about it." When we watch the news we see horror stories being played out in real life. We live in a world where sin runs rampant and it seems to be more prevalent each day. We know as Christians that there is an eternal darkness as well. What a sad and scary thought this would be if we didn't have God's assurance. Where would we be headed without Christ to redeem us? Way before we were born, God provided a way for us to be delivered from this evil. It gets even better because God transported us into a place of redemption. We may be affected by what happens on this earth, but we have eternal redemption through Christ!

What wonderful news God that You have transported us to redemption. Thank You that we do not have to fear the evils of this world because of who we are in You.

LOVE

Deuteronomy 6:5

You shall love the LORD your God with all your heart, with all your soul, and with all your strength.

I think of all of the verses in the Bible, this is one of the simplest ones. Now, I didn't say that it was the easiest one or the one that all of us Christians excel at. It's a commandment, straight and simple. Why shouldn't it be easy for us to love God? After all, He did love us first and let's admit it - He also loved us most! You know in your heart that He did something for us that you and I most likely would never do. Okay, what about love Him with all our heart? That means with all of the love that you can muster up. Let's say like the love you have for your child or grandchild. The love that encompasses everything else. The commandment takes it a step further. With all of your soul, now that might be easier. I believe that since God created our soul that only He can live in it. So what about with all of your strength? Since we can't physically touch God I have to believe that this means our mental and emotional strength. We can physically show Him that we love Him by reading and sharing His word, by keeping His commandments and living each day for Him.

Father, help us today to give You our love and praise. Thank You for the gift of Your salvation and the many blessings that You give us each day.

MIRACLE

Deuteronomy 10:21

He is your praise, and He is your God, who has done for you these great and awesome things which your eyes have seen.

I know that we see God at work all of the time, each new day He brings us, a new baby being born and so many other beautiful things that He has allowed us to experience. When I think about all of these things, I can't help but think how it must have been to live in Biblical times. Those people saw with their own eyes God revealing himself through Jesus. Think about some of the things that Christ did while He was here on earth. Can you imagine being at the wedding in Cana when Jesus performed His first miracle and turned the water into wine? He was just beginning to reveal Himself as God's Son and that should have made people stop and take notice. I think about the times He healed the lame, the blind and those sick unto death. He even raised Lazarus from the dead! He did great and awesome things in Biblical times and He is still at work doing great and awesome things! He was their God during Biblical times and He is our God today. Open your eyes and look!

Thank You Lord for the things that we see of beauty that You supply for us and thank You for the many things that You provide that we cannot see and accept on faith.

ASSURANCE

Jeremiah 29:11

For I know the thoughts that I think toward you, says the LORD, thoughts of peace and not of evil, to give you a future and a hope.

This is probably one of the most quoted verses from the Bible. I know a lot of times when problems arise among us, we pull this scripture out to cling too. It is such a reassuring scripture. Don't you find it amazing and overwhelming that our great big God can be so personal? I mean He's talking to us! He's telling us that He is thinking about us and that He wants good for us. I don't think I will ever get over the fact that He loves me. Little me with all of my faults and failings. It's so humbling to think that the Creator of the universe cares enough about me to make sure that I know it. He cares when I'm sick or upset or hurt. He cares when my world is in shambles. He cares about what I care about! I can't help but think how much this verse exemplifies the character of a parent right here. Growing up there were certain things I never doubted. One of them was my parents love for me. They wanted what was good for me and they wanted me to have a future. They worked hard to provide for me and to meet my physical needs. They provided an education for me so that it would help secure my future. They surely must have been modeling after God to want those things for me.

Thank You Father for thinking of us each day, for providing a way for us to go forward with hope for our future.

Foundation

Deuteronomy 32:4

He is the Rock, His work is perfect; For all His ways are justice, A God of truth and without injustice; Righteous and upright is He.

"On Christ the solid rock I stand, all other ground is sinking sand!" I love the words to this old hymn. This verse makes me think of those words. I'm also reminded of that little song we use to sing in Vacation Bible School about building on the rock or the sand. If we build our foundation upon The Rock, the One Whose ways are perfect and just then how can we go wrong? There are so many of us and I mean Christians looking for something, and so many times we are looking in the wrong places. We may be saved from hell but are we relying on God to show us the way each day? He will never lead us down the wrong path because His paths are righteous paths. Begin each day with your feet planted on the Solid Rock!

Thank You Lord for being our Rock! Thank You for letting our foundation be solid in You.

FRUIT OF THE SPIRIT

Galatians 5:22- 23

But the fruit of the Spirit is love, joy, peace, longsuffering, kindness, goodness, faithfulness, gentleness, self-control. Against such there is no law.

This is a well know Bible verse and one we may feel that we take to heart. I know in my heart what the verse means. However, I really don't think I practice it every day. I have a feeling if we spent just a little bit of time dissecting this verse we could find out a lot more about it. The Spirit, being God, means that we should display love, joy, peace, and longsuffering like God. See how the wording can make you rethink the meaning. So if we are to have God's spirit in us then we should be able to practice loving like He does. Wow! You might say, but He's God, it's easy for Him to love, He's supposed to love. So are we! We are supposed to have peace and joy, we should show kindness and goodness and have a gentle nature. Yes, we should exhibit self-control and long suffering. We know that doing all of these things is a tall order and even doing part of them is difficult sometimes, We must remember that God wants us to show others about Him. In order to show God's love we must have it in us to share.

Lord, this seems like such a hard task sometimes. Help us to grow more like You so that we can reach others for You.

WORSHIP

Psalm 92:1

It is a good thing to give thanks unto the Lord, and to sing praises unto thy name, o most high.

A friend of mine had this saying. "You should praise God the most when you feel like praising Him the least". Tonight I've been frustrated in general and just out of sorts. There are so many little things in and around me that I have no control over and I hate not having control over stuff! It just makes me ill! Instead of stewing and fussing, I should be praising my Lord for all of His blessings and all of the things that are right in my life! So you see, I guess that saying is true! While I am blowing up about the little things that I can't control I could be looking around and seeing all of the other things that I should be grateful for. Why is it so easy to be out of sorts over stuff that won't even matter a year from now, or maybe even a month from now? I guess that just makes me human. I'm so thankful that even while I'm all stressed out about the small stuff, God is still blessing me in big ways! It's certainly not that I deserve His blessings and certainly not because I praised Him in the midst of the stress, it's just because He loves me so much! He wants me to let Him have control of all of the "stuff" in my life.

Thank You God that I have so much to praise You for and thank You God that even when my life seems upside down or inside out that I can still praise Your precious name.

Working

Ephesians 2:8-9

For by **grace** you have been saved through faith, and that not of yourselves; *it is* the gift of God, not of works, lest anyone should boast.

Are you an ant? These tiny insects are workers. If you study the species you will find that they work tirelessly every day. We tend to do that in our Christian lives. We just work away at being a good Christian! Now don't get me wrong, God expects us to work for Him. In fact it's biblical to carry out God's work. We just need to remember that it is God's grace that saves us, not anything that we do for Him or anything that we do in the church. It's our faith that leads us to believe in God and His grace that perfects that faith. That grace is a gift from God and nothing you ever do can be enough to pay for it or earn it. You must accept it freely with the faith of a child and then children you go to work. Not for your glory but for God's glory and as a way to give back to His work. It's okay to be an ant as long as you know whose hill you belong to.

God, thank You for the many opportunities to work for You. We know God that You want Your children to be working for You until Your glorious return.

WEAK

Hebrews 2:18

For in that He Himself has suffered, being tempted, He is able to aid those who are tempted.

How weak our earthly bodies are and how easy it is to be tempted and pulled away from God's ways. Satan always will catch us at our weakest moment. He will always use our greatest insecurities to tempt us. He uses cunning lies to sell his ways to you. He goes about undermining that which is good and holy. He waits for us to let our guard down just an inch and then he pounces! When Jesus was on the mountain top and had gone 40 days without food or water, the devil showed up. He knew that Jesus in His human body was hungry and thirsty and probably physically weak. Satan proceeded to offer food, water and a way to get out of the situation that Jesus was in.

Jesus held firm in His convictions, knowing who His Master was and knowing that God was going to take care of Him. When you are working for Christ and doing the best you know how to please Him is when you are making the devil the maddest. He will seize those moments to try and de-rail your plans to serve God. Stay strong as Jesus stayed strong by keeping your focus on the Father.

God, how many times I have failed You, how often have I let the devil win? It grieves my heart to think that I was so weak. Please help us to stand strong in our faith against the ways of the enemy.

INTERVENTION

Isaiah 38:5

"Go and tell Hezekiah, 'Thus says the LORD, the God of David your father: "I have heard your prayer, I have seen your tears; surely I will add to your days fifteen years."

I love this verse for two reasons. First God is reassuring Hezekiah that He has heard his prayers. Secondly, He lets Hezekiah know that He saw his tears. I bet you can't begin to name all of the prayers that you've prayed to God. I imagine that with those prayers like Hezekiah, you've shed some tears along the way. I know people that have consistently prayed for a situation for years, often begging God for a resolution. Many times, I've found myself on my knees before God, tears streaming down my face, praying for divine intervention. Praying for healing or restoration. In this case Hezekiah didn't want to die, so he prayed that God might lengthen his life. God heard his prayer and granted his petition. We must have faith that God is hearing our prayers even when we don't immediately get an answer. We must wait for God to act and to grant answers to our prayers in His time.

Thank You Father God that You answer our prayers right on time.

Pure

1 John 3:5

And ye know that he was manifested to take away our sins; and in him is no sin.

As I sit here and look out my window, I see fresh beautiful snow on every surface. I live in the South and so to be able to see six or more inches of snow is amazing. I've always loved to watch it snow and watching it for about twelve hours yesterday reminded me of its purity. When I think about purity I think about Christ and how pure He was when He came to this earth and how pure He remained the thirty three years that He lived here as a man. When you look up the word *pure*, you find the words "spotless, containing nothing that does not properly belong." That is what God sent to us, something pure that would eliminate our sins. Jesus had to be pure in order to die for our sins. The next time that you see snow falling stop just a moment and thank God for His Son, pure as the driven snow.

Thank You God for sending us Your spotless pure son so that we might one day stand before You, our creator as pure and white as snow.

COMPLETE

Colossians 2:10

And ye are complete in him, which is the head of all principality and power.

I'm a list maker! I seem to operate better when I can make a list and check items off of it as I get them done. I went to work really early today to try to complete a few things on my "to do" list. Each time I would finish a project and put it aside I would think COMPLETE! It always feels great to complete a project and not have to go back to it. I love the note in my Bible about this verse: "Nothing can be added to completeness." Jesus did an eternal work for us and in our lives! Jesus completed a work for us! HE died for us and because of this we have completeness in HIM. Don't you love it? Aren't you thankful? I AM!

God in Heaven, Thank You so much for doing a work in my life, an eternal work. I am so amazed that You care about me and my life. Help me to lead others to find completeness through You.

WORDS OF ANGER

Psalm 19:14

Let the words of my mouth and the meditation of my heart, Be acceptable in Your sight, O LORD, my strength and my Redeemer.

I use to have a quick and ugly temper. Thankfully, as I have grown in my Christian life God has removed most of it. It's easy for those ugly remarks to fly out of our mouths and they can do so much damage. We all know that once it's said, there is no taking it back. No matter how badly we feel, after the fact the words are spoken and have made their mark. A great friend of mine used this quote all of time. "What's in your well comes out your bucket." That quote has saved me from opening my mouth and spewing out ugliness many times! After all, if Christ is in my well, then Christ should be coming out of my bucket! Maybe that is what God wanted us to know from this scriptures - that it is important what we hold in our hearts. We want others to see Jesus in us, but we must have Him in us completely for it to be real and to show. It's easy for the right things to come out of our mouths at church or maybe work, but think about those other places we go. The grocery store, the ballpark, the hairdresser. Are we letting our words be acceptable to our Redeemer? Fill your bucket up with the right things and then the right things will come out of your bucket!

God thank You for taking away the ugliness of my temper. Thank You that I can find other ways to express anger when the time comes. Thank You for filling my bucket with Your words.

Shield

Psalm 28:7

The Lord is my strength and my shield; My heart trusted in Him, and I am helped; Therefore my heart greatly rejoices, And with my song I will praise Him.

When I hear the word strength, I envision someone big and brawny. When I think about the word *shield*, I think about protection. I think about a knight in armor wearing a shield to protect himself. A shield is not penetrable. So when I put those two words together like they are in this verse I get a picture of a warrior. A strong and mighty warrior! Well, I guess I shouldn't be surprised because after all God is our Warrior. He's our Protector! He takes care of His, because we belong to Him. He stands between us and the devil and guards us from the evils of this world. We know that Satan has been defeated. We know that no harm can come to us when we trust in God. We should leap with joy every day just knowing that our great big God is protecting us all of the time. Will you praise Him today for his protection?

Thank You Lord for Your divine protection! Thank You for being our Mighty Warrior!

HEALED

Isaiah 53:5

But he [was] wounded for our transgressions, [he was] bruised for our iniquities: the chastisement of our peace [was] upon him; and with his stripes we are healed.

With His stripes we are healed! Do you notice anything significant about this verse? All of the other statements were past tense. He was! Then in the last sentence of this verse, we find our hope. We find because He suffered, bled and died that we are eternally healed! Far too many of my friends have said earthly goodbyes to their children. I've prayed alongside many of them as they claimed this verse as their very own. They claimed it because their faith in Jesus is strong. That's a lot of faith folks. It takes a strong Christian to have the kind of faith to claim this verse no matter the outcome. They trusted God whether He chose to heal their child right here on earth or to heal them eternally. We are forever healed with his blood that poured out of those stripes when He was beaten. He withstood that pain for us so that we wouldn't have to withstand it ourselves.

God, I'm so humbled when I read this verse to think about how You suffered. I can't imagine loving someone as much as You loved us when You took our beatings and our transgressions. Saying thank You will never be good enough to express my feelings of gratitude for all You have done and continue doing for me.

EMPTINESS

Ephesians 3:17-19

Christ may dwell in your hearts by faith; that you, being rooted and grounded in love, may be able to comprehend... the fullness of God.

What are you looking for? Don't we all get so caught up in what we want or what we think we need? What we really need is Jesus! We tend to think that other things will fill that place of emptiness in our hearts. I've heard references to "the God shaped hole in our heart". I believe it's true that we all have a place in our heart that only God can fill and that nothing else will fit there correctly. We will eventually find that nothing the world offers will fill that space. We must look toward filling our hearts with something that will last throughout eternity! We have to think about filling our hearts with our Master. We have to believe that we are created by Him for Him and that we will not have true contentment or peace without Him being the center of all that we do. We were created to serve Him, He wants us to accept who He is in our lives and become His servant in doing His work. Open up your heart today and let Jesus come in. Your life will be so much sweeter!

God thank You so much that You live in my heart! Thank You that You filled the hole in my heart many years ago.

Giving

2 Corinthians 9: 7

So let each one give as he purposes in his heart, not grudgingly or of necessity; for God loves a cheerful giver.

When we think of tithing we automatically think of money, but I believe that in this verse God was talking about more than just how much money we drop in the plate on Sunday mornings. Yes it is important for us to give money to our church. It's used in many places to fulfill various needs. We have to pay the power bill and water bill. We have to be able to pay our pastor's salary and the staff who serve us so well. This is just a small part of stewardship. We can give of our time and our talents. Yes, you do have a talent! Maybe you haven't discovered it yet, but if you will start praying about it, God will show it to you. As far as giving time, you may be thinking that you don't have any time left to give to anything. Then maybe you need to reprioritize your time. We seem to have time in our lives for who and what we think is important. Pray and ask God to show you what He wants you to do with your time. Believe me when you start asking God to guide you in the three T's: tithing, talents and time, you will start to see opportunities open up. Be a cheerful giver of all that God has given you!

God, please allow us to see giving in a new way. Help us to be willing to give of our time and talents that You have blessed us with.

Fear

Deuteronomy 31:8

"And the Lord. He it is that doth go before thee' He will be with thee, He will not fail thee, either forsake thee: Fear not, neither be dismayed."

A gripping fear came upon me this morning at 4:50 when my cell phone rang. You know the one that sends your heart racing and puts your mind in a fog. It was our security network stating that the fire department was on the way due to a smoke alarm signal being detected in our home. We jumped out of bed, searching and smelling for smoke or fire in our home. The fire department which in our community is volunteer, shows up and does a look around the exterior. Thankfully, it seems to be a false alarm. The first thing I think about is sitting down to write this, maybe because in a crisis or a possible one the first place my mind and heart go is to my Creator. He knows all things and He is in control of all things. Could I have sat down and written this had there been a fire? If things had turned out for the worse? I certainly hold true to believing that I would have. I have to believe that my faith in God and in this verse would stay strong regardless of the outcome. Where do you go when you need your fears calmed? Who's the first person you cry out to when things go wrong? God created us in His likeness. He loves us and will protect us and calm our fears no matter what the situation.

Lord, thank You so much for Your divine protection! Thank You that You know my fears and You know how to calm them.

Rock

I Samuel 2:2

There is none holy as the LORD: for *there is* none beside thee: neither *is there* any rock like our God.

Just the other day I was speaking to a sweet friend of mine and she told me that I was her rock. Naturally, that was humbling to me to think that she feels that way about me. My response to her was that I hoped that I had consistently pointed her toward the real rock. The rock that will not crumble no matter what she is going through. The one that she can lean on and rely on forever. That unshakable rock is our Creator, our Lord and Savior. Yes he is my rock and I am honored to lead others to lean on Him as well. Is He your rock? Can you place all of your cares on Him and know that He will not let you down. He is the cornerstone of Christianity. Jesus the rock that will stand firm throughout all eternity!

Lord, thank You so much for being my rock! Thank You for allowing me to be strong for my friends and to point them to You!

Respect

Exodus 20:17

Thou shalt not take the name of the LORD thy God in vain; for the LORD will not hold him guiltless that taketh his name in vain.

I don't think there is anything that upsets me more than to hear a person use my Savior's name as a curse. It seems that even children use His name as slang. Turn on the television or go to a movie and you will hear His name used in vain. What I can't seem to get past is that they are degrading our Creator! The King of Kings and Lord of Lords! They have so little respect for Him that they can integrate His name with filthy words. How can we Christians stand by and let this happen? How can we partake in it? How can we accept it? There have been times that I have absolutely asked a person to stop using God's name in that way. I take this very personally and know that I must be bolder in speaking out against it no matter who might be using His name in an inappropriate way. His name is to be revered and lifted up and it is up to us to make sure that it is not defamed!

Father God, how majestic is Your name! Help us God to be bold and stand up when Your name is being torn down.

Help

Psalm 121:1-2

I lift up my eyes to the hills, from where does my help come? My help comes from the Lord, who made heaven and earth.

Who does your help come from? Wait!! Don't answer yet! Think about the question for a few minutes. When my mother was still alive she was my "go to" person when anything happened. To be honest she was probably the first one that I would turn to, even before God. That wasn't an intentional decision. If you have or had a close relationship with your parents you probably understand. I have to believe that God didn't mind as He gave her such wisdom to direct me in my times of need. My hope is as a parent we are always leading our children to seek God and ask for His help first. I find I seek Him more, on a regular basis for every need in my life. Maybe that comes with growing older, I'd like to believe that it means maturing as a Christian. One thing I know for sure my help has, does and always will come from the Lord!

Thank You Father for being there for me every time that I've called on You. Thank You for showing me the wisdom of Your ways.

Train

Proverbs 22: 6

Train up a child in the way he should go: and when he is old, he will not depart from it.

As parents we spend a lot of time training our children to do particular tasks. If you think about it, a child's training begins with the first breath they take after being born. We begin cooing and talking with them introducing them to their first sounds, they learn to take a bottle and pacifier and so on. Further down the road they are potty trained. It is our duty as parents to make sure that they are prepared for what life brings them. How much time do we put into spiritual training? It should begin at birth as well. We should make sure that we are spending time talking about God with our children. Yes, even when they are babies. We should take them to church and expose them to other Christian activities. Bedtime prayers and before meal blessings should be incorporated into our daily lives. Children are like little sponges soaking up what they are exposed to. Don't you want your child to soak up a love for their Creator and be led to Christ while they are young? While their hearts are still soft and tender, help ready them for salvation.

God help us to remember the most important training for Your children is that of spiritual training. Let us as parent be quick to use teachable moments to lead our children to You and Your word.

LIGHT

Psalm 27: 1

The Lord is my light and my salvation; whom shall I fear? The Lord is the strength of my life; of whom shall I be afraid?

When you were a child perhaps you were afraid of the dark, or maybe you were afraid of a monster under your bed. Most likely when you grew up you realized that there were no real monsters under the bed and that the dark wasn't that scary after all. Those were just childhood fears. As adults we still have fears. Some of those fears are very real, maybe due to circumstances in your life. Some of us have fears that to others seem ludicrous. However, if you're the person with those fears, they are very real to you. Some of us may fear financial ruin, others of us may fear our spouse leaving us, or our children turning away from us. We may have a fear of growing old or dying. God gave us so many promises in His word. He gave us verses to reassure us, to comfort us, to chastise us. He gave us this verse to allay our fears! Whom shall I fear? No one! That's what this verse is saying. I believe that God gave us this verse so that we are reminded that He is always with us and that no fear that we can possibly have is greater than He is.

Lord, we are so thankful for Your promise of protection. We thank You that no fear can be greater than Your love and protection for us.

THIRST

John 4:14

But whosoever drinketh of the water that I shall give him shall never thirst: but the water I shall give him shall be in him a well of water springing up into everlasting life.

Have you ever worked in the garden or the yard on a hot summer day? Have you ever been to the ballpark to watch your kids play or to the golf course for a round of golf on a dry humid day? You know that parched feeling you get? So thirsty. You can't seem to think about anything else except getting a cool refreshing drink of water. In today's world we are constantly carrying around our water bottles with us. I even see folks in churches, and work places, water bottles close at hand. When we go out to restaurants we often are treated to free refills which we take full advantage of. It seems we are a thirsty bunch. Have you ever drank and not had your thirst quenched? In this scripture it says we will never thirst again. When this scripture was first given, people marveled at how that could be. They were thinking about being physically thirsty. God, however, was talking about our well being dry. He was talking about us being spiritually parched! He gives us living water that continues to flow and will continually quench our thirst. Have you had a drink from the well of Jesus?

Father, thank You for quenching our thirst continually, Thank You for giving us relief for our parched souls.

Golden Rule

Luke 6:31

And as ye would that men should do to you, do ye also to them likewise.

All of my life I've heard this quoted. At home, at school and at church. I don't know when I realized that it wasn't just random words, but that it was God's words to us. He knew if He made it personal we would understand it better. We would understand the idea of someone treating us well. We all want to be treated with respect and kindness. Admit it, we want others to think well of us and to feel we are an upstanding citizen of our communities. We all want to be loved, cherished and understood. I think about what being good to one another really means. As Christians we should be lifting each other up in prayer, being a good neighbor and helping out when someone needs it. To me being good to someone entails more than just being amicable, it means truly caring about another person. Let's take this old quote to heart and put feet on it every day!

Father thank You for giving us this scripture, thank You for engraining it into us as children.

WITNESS

Joshua 1: 9

Have I not commanded you? Be strong and courageous. Do not be frightened, and do not be dismayed, for the Lord your God is with you wherever you go.

Are you afraid to witness? It's not always easy to tell others about our faith in God. I really wonder why that is. We all have a network of friends that we are comfortable with and I bet we have no problem talking with them about Christ. In fact, it's easy to talk with a fellow Christian about our faith. It's when I hear that little small voice in my head and my heart saying "that person needs to hear about Me" that I freeze up. How on earth do I begin a conversation about God with a complete stranger? It may be difficult at first but I believe just like the scripture tells us that God will give us the words. I just have to take that first step of faith in obeying God and what He is asking me to do. I've seldom had anyone that I approached stop me or be rude to me. Actually, most of the times I've stepped up and talked about my faith, people have thanked me. A lot of times when I've begun to share my faith I would find out that the person was already a believer. God may have sent me just because they needed a reminder of His love that day. Maybe God just wanted me to be willing. Are you willing?

Father, help me to be courageous when an opportunity to witness for You comes about. Give me the boldness when You tell me to go tell others about You. Give me the words that You would have me speak and guide my steps.

FORGIVE

Colossians 3:13

Bear with each other and forgive one another if any of you has a grievance against someone. Forgive as the Lord forgave you.

I know sometimes it's hard to bear with one another. Especially when someone seems to be attacking or undermining you. Anytime that I have the feeling that I am not living out this verse I start thinking about God's forgiveness. When I'm unforgiving toward someone, I start thinking about how God forgave me. More importantly I think about what forgiving us cost Him. His Son had to die to accomplish it. Many people waste years of their lives with unforgiving attitudes. I know people that have held grudges for years, I've watched it turn them into bitter people. Maybe that is why I cannot hold a grudge. I normally don't stay angry very long. I only have to think about my Heavenly Father forgiving me to humble myself to the point of forgiveness.

Father, if not for Your forgiveness we would be lost and going to hell. Thank You God that You forgave all of our sins and gave us an amazing example of forgiveness.

HUMBLE

Psalm 25:9

The humble He guides in justice, And the humble He teaches His way.

Humility, doesn't it make someone so beautiful to you? How many people do you know that are humble? I can only name 5 or 6 people that strike me as truly humble. They have a meek spirit. They have a soft voice and they don't try to stand out or draw attention to themselves. Instead, they show this sweet and gentle spirit that must come from their relationship with Christ. They have opinions and sometimes strong ones, but the way they deliver those opinions are gentle. They seem to be full of compassion and are slow to judge others. I've also found that they seek God in all of their endeavors. It is with a love for others that they share Christ. Some of my best mentors and friends in my life have been those with a humble heart. I learned so much from the way they conduct themselves in life's situations. We need to pattern ourselves after Christ and be humble.

Father, remind us to have a meek and humble spirit and remind us that we must get this from You.

SUPPLICATION

Psalm 6:9

The LORD hath heard my supplication; the LORD will receive my prayer.

Prayer is our lifeline to God, yes He hears our prayers! All of them! It's how we communicate with Him. It shouldn't be a time for us to just throw our request at Him and take off. If the truth be told among us I imagine that many of us tend to do that. When is the last time that you knelt in prayer? I'm talking about getting down on your knees and humbling yourself before your Creator? We usually do this when our business is serious; when we are in need of a real touch from our Father. How about thanking Him? Do you take the time to thank Him for loving you, for listening to you and for answering the prayers you've already prayed! Do you tell Him you love Him? That you adore him? That you will place no other God before Him? You see all of these are aspects of prayer (communicating with God). You don't always have to be formal with your prayers either. Quite often I send up a quick little prayer, just a few words, I pray on my way to work some days. It's not about the place or the length of the prayer to me, it is just making the time to submit myself to God each day. I just want to give Him honor and glory before I start my day. Starting my day by giving Him the lead is the best possible way to start my day.

Thank You Lord so much for the opportunity to pray. Thank You for giving us this way to communicate with You.

GROWTH

John 15:5

I am the vine, ye are the branches: He that abideth in me, and I in him, the same bringeth forth much fruit: for without me ye can do nothing.

Have you ever grown a garden? You dig a hole in the ground, put your little seed in the hole, water it a little bit and then cover it with dirt and wait for it to grow. You've invested a little bit of time into planting that seed. It begins to grow up from the ground and before long has sprouted little green branches. Now if you cut one of those branches off of the main plant it will wither and die. God is our main plant. We are His little soft tender branches. We can grow only if we stay connected to Him as our life source. We can not only grow ourselves but we can produce fruit from our little branch. We can begin to produce seeds of our own so that they can be planted and grow new branches. We can bring forth fruit for our Father when we are fed with His word.

Father, thank You so much for being our Vine, thank You for allowing us to grow in You and to plant seeds of hope and love in others.

UNITY

Matthew 18:20

For where two or three are gathered together in my name,
there am I in the midst of them.

All of my life I have heard there is safety in numbers, take a buddy with you when you go swimming or on a hike. Boy Scouts teach the buddy system for a reason. It's because you are better and bigger and stronger together than you are alone. Why should this be any different in our Christian life? When we are weak and need support we can go to our close friends and our family member, but why stop there? Take them with you and go to your Father who created you. As Christians one of the things that we do naturally and quickly when tragedy strikes is to unite. We gather together to pray, to offer spiritual support and meals. We step in to make sure that the person's life can continue in the day to day realm while they are dealing with the fallout of tragedy. This is taught by God, He wants us to gather together and minister to others. He is always going to be right there guiding and directing our steps. The next time that you know of someone going through the fires of this world, walk with them awhile and ask that our Father walk along side of you both. He will be in the midst of it all.

God, this verse is so true in my life, when I go back and think about the bleakest times in my life, I have sweet memories of my friends and church family walking along side of me. Those times were when I felt Your presence in a very real way.

Church

Hebrews 10:25

Not forsaking the assembling of ourselves together, as the manner of some [is]; but exhorting [one another]: and so much the more, as ye see the day approaching.

Why do we go to church? I know that for myself, I need that time during the week to gain fortification for the days ahead. I go to church so that I can have my spiritual cup refilled. However, our going to church says a lot about our walk with God. It says that we want to be together to worship our King. It shows others that we realize that we must depend upon Him to strengthen us to move forward. Attending church is a non-verbal witness. Our friends and co-workers may not see us going to church but I bet they hear us talk about going. At my house it isn't a decision as to whether or not we are going to church, it's something that we just do. God calls us to go to church out of devotion to Him, He teaches us to assemble ourselves together to edify one another. When I am at church I am with fellow believers that love God. We are there to give back some of our time, money and talents to Him. I am so thankful that we live in a country where we can go to the house of the Lord without fear. When we attend church we are saying to the world I believe in God! I Love my Savior!

Thank You Lord for my church family. I am so blessed to be a part of Your work in our church.

SAILING

Isaiah 40:31

But they that wait upon the Lord shall renew their strength; they shall mount up with wings as eagles; they shall run, and not be weary; and they shall walk and not faint.

We have a lake not too far from my home where you can find eagles nesting. When I was younger my dad would take me there to find their nest and observe those beautiful birds. Occasionally, we would see one take flight and glide effortlessly across the sky. I think back about seeing those majestic birds sailing so carefree into the horizon. I have always loved this verse; it is such a verse of assurance and hope. We can sail like eagles free from our burdens and cares. We don't have to be weary in our doings because God has strengthened us. He has given us the energy to continue on even when we feel like we are trudging in mud. I just picture us taking wings and flying high above all that consumes us, dropping off our burdens and being free from all of our cares. God will continue to come to us and give us what we need the most, and re-fill our spirits. We will not faint because we serve a God that wants us to fly to our highest potential and fulfill our hearts desires. His love will not fail you and He will give you wings!

Thank You God for renewing my strength day by day, thank You for giving me what I need to continue on this journey.

Friends

John 15:15

Henceforth I call you not servants; for the servant knoweth not what his lord doeth: but I have called you friends; for all things that I have heard of my Father I have made known unto you.

We all have friends, some of them may be very close friends and some may be casual friends. I imagine that we all have a few friends that know everything about us, all of our deep dark secrets and our true heart. After all we are our real true selves with our best friends. We don't try to mask who or what we are from them. Can you imagine having this kind of relationship with Jesus? I try to picture in my mind what it must have been like for the disciples to walk on this earth with Him. They knew Jesus intimately and He knew them that way as well. There wasn't anything that Jesus didn't share with them, His friends. This verse always makes me think of that old church hymn "what a friend we have in Jesus." He truly is not just our Savior, our Creator, our Redeemer or our Comforter, but he is our Friend. He knows our hearts and we are allowed to know His. What a beautiful thing to be able to sit down and talk to my Savior as my friend.

Lord, thank You so much for being my friend! I can't even fathom the love You have for me.

Calvary

John 19: 18

There they crucified him, and with him two others, one on either side, with Jesus in the middle.

I've heard it preached that the day that our Savior died on the cross was the darkest day of all humanity. Crucifixion was the way that people were put to death who did not observe the Roman laws. Crucifixion was the most painful, longest, degrading death that a person could suffer. It was meant to tear down the respect others had for that person, it was meant to set the person as an example of wrongdoing. Even as Jesus hung on the cross, one of the two that hung beside Him cursed him. As He hung there onlookers jeered at Him and called Him names. Since He had been portrayed as the son of God, they shouted for Him to save Himself. I have to believe that in these moments is when our Savior was the meekest. He withstood physical anguish that words can't describe. He was spat upon and ridiculed. In His final hours He prayed for the very ones that hung him on the cross. Our Savior went through all of this for us! Jesus stretched out his arms on the cross to say I love you this much.

God in heaven, how it rips my heart out to think of Your precious Son beaten and bleeding and dying for me. How much You loved me to allow Him to suffer in that way. Father, I can never be good enough to repay that debt and I'm so thankful that I don't have to be. I'm so thankful that because Your Son took my sin I can receive Your grace and be saved from hell.

Guide

Revelation 21:6

And he said unto me, It is done. I am Alpha and Omega, the beginning and the end. I will give unto him that is athirst of the fountain of the water of life freely.

This week after attending the funeral of a sweet saint in our church I was led to this verse. It may not be a verse we hear read much at funerals, but it means something special to me. God finishes as well as he begins. He begins a work in us and he will see it performed. What more can we ask for as Christians? We know that if He lives in us and we walk with Him, He will be with us always. When we leave this earthly body and gain our Heavenly one, Jesus will have perfected His grace in us. At the end of our lives we will acquire that water of life because we let Him quench our thirst throughout our lifetime. When we depend on God to be our guide during our lives, then we can be assured that our final rest will be in Him. Are you ready to begin with God so that you can end with Him?

Lord, what an amazing promise that You have given us. You have promised us in Your word that even as You were with us at birth that You will be with us in death. I am so thankful for Your promise.

DECISIONS

Matthew 6:24

No man can serve two masters: for either he will hate the one, and love the other; or else he will hold to the one, and despise the other. Ye cannot serve God and mammon.

When I was growing up in a rural area we had cattle and horses. A lot of our land was fenced in to house them. Many times I either crawled under the fence or pinched the top of the fence down and crawled over it. The one thing I learned early on is you couldn't "straddle the fence" without being injured. This phrase was used often in our town when referring to choosing a side to support on a given subject. You could either be for it or against it but you couldn't "straddle the fence." As Christians we can't "straddle the fence" either, we must choose a side. If we are serving Christ and living for Him then we should have clear views on sin. We should be able to recognize sin immediately and walk away from it. In today's world the lines between right and wrong are being blurred and we are being told to accept things we know are sinful. We may not be able to control the legalization of some of these things but we can control our own personal beliefs on the subject. We should not condone sin. We must take our stand for Christ and hold true to our beliefs.

Father, we know that You want us to separate ourselves from sin. We don't understand how the lines can get so blurred for us and our leaders. We know that sin will always have consequences according to Your word. We ask that You keep us strong in Your word so that we might not sin against You.

IDOLS

Exodus 20:3

You shall have no other gods before Me.

How many god's do you have other than God? What? Now I know that you are saying you don't have anything that you place before God in your life. I bet if you are honest with yourself you will realize you do. I find in my own life it's not even important things that take my time away from God. Its things like being on social media sites, watching television, etc. For you it may be a sport that you or your child are involved in. It may be some hobby that you enjoy. Don't get me wrong, sports and hobbies are all good things in a person's life. The problem lies when they become more important than your relationship with God. The things of the world so readily catch our attention and pull us away from God. We must stay diligent in our quest for Godly activities which keep us in line with the scripture and what God wants for our lives.

Lord, please help us to keep our minds on what really matters. Helps us to stay focused on You in all things and not to have any other gods.

SACRIFICE

Romans 5:8

But God commendeth his love toward us, in that, while we were yet sinners, Christ died for us.

Christ died for us! Can you even wrap your head around this sentence? Christians tend to tuck that into our beliefs with very little thought. Do we realize that God, in his wisdom, sent us a Savior, in the form of a baby, watched Him grow into a fleshly human being, watched Him be ridiculed, spit upon and ultimately crucified for us! We know that Christ was the blood sacrifice for us, the only one that could have died to forgive our sins eternally and secure a home in Heaven for us. Could you do it? Think about it! Could you give yourself as a sacrifice to save others? On September 11th, 2001, the passengers of United Flight 93 headed for Washington, DC, did exactly that, to save countless others that would have been affected. Let's go one step further. Could you give up your child? Could you watch your child be born, glorified and honored, and then die to save others? These are hard questions. The one's that make us squirm in our seats when the preacher talks about it. These are the ones that we need to think about when we take what God did for us lightly!

God thank You so much that You didn't ask us to give up our loved ones. Thank You for giving Your precious son for us.

COMPASSION

Lamentations 3:22

It is of the LORD's mercies that we are not consumed, because his compassions fail not.

Are you compassionate? Do you know people that are not compassionate? Sometimes it's difficult to have compassion for others. Often times we find that people confuse compassion with pity. Some people revel in feeling sorry for themselves. It's easy to throw a great big pity party for ourselves. Sometimes, I think that I am not very compassionate, then other times I think I tend to be too caring. I like to fix things for people, and I like to think I can fix people! I've found through the years that the best possible thing I can do to help people fix things or to help fix people is to point them to the Healer of all things. You see He is always compassionate; He cares for you and about what happens to you and your family.

Thank You God for Your caring spirit. Thank You for giving us Your tender loving care at all times.

Struggles

1 John 4:4

Ye are of God, little children, and have overcome them: because greater is he that is in you, than he that is in the world.

Right now my family is going through some serious struggles. I feel like the devil has me on re-dial and that he keeps punching it! Thankfully, this verse is just what I need to remember to keep me grounded. How often do we find ourselves in the middle of turmoil and start wringing our hands in despair? The way we handle struggles when we go through them may be the best testimony of our faith. Others see us staying strong in our faith when things aren't going smoothly and depending on God's promises to carry us through no matter what. We can do that because God promised us that we could! He promised us that we already have victory over this world and its problems. All of them! Are you claiming this promise for the struggles you are going through? Are you clinging to God's promises? He won't let you down!

Father, I need You so much right now to calm my fears and to fight my battles for me. Thank You that I know You are willing and able to do that for me.

JOY

Psalm 30:5

For his anger endureth but a moment; in his favour is life: weeping may endure for a night, but joy cometh in the morning.

Joy! Do you have joy in your heart? Are you joyful? You cannot experience joy without God! Yes, I know that we can feel joyous when something wonderful happens. The joy I'm speaking about is that deep down joy that doesn't depend on your circumstances. This joy isn't a feeling, it's a condition. Your heart is joyful because God came into your heart and cleaned it up and gave you HIS joy! This joy will supersede everyday trails. This joy will continually grow in your heart with God as its source! This joy will spill over onto others as you go about your day. It is this joy that will endure and overcome!

Thank You God for Your promise of eternal joy! Thank You that no matter what our circumstances are right now, we will experience Your joy!

Time

Psalm 119:77

Let thy tender mercies come unto me, that I may live: for thy law [is] my delight.

How much time do you spend in God's word? Do you take a few moments each day to acknowledge Him in your life? We want God to notice us, we expect Him to take care of us. We expect Him to always be available and He is. He wants us to be available to Him as well; He wants our hearts to be in tune with Him. We can do this by studying His word, (the law). We can be ready for whatever He has for us when we stay in touch with Him. We know that in relationships that we grow closer together by being together, doing things together. Moments spent together enrich our relationship. This is true with our relationship with Christ as well. Spend some time with your Creator today!

God help us to not be so busy that we forget You! Let us come to You each day with awe and wonder at who You are in our life.

STEADFASTNESS

Hebrews 13:8

Jesus Christ the same yesterday and today, and forever.

I praise the Lord for this verse! In an ever-changing world it is so awesome to have God's word that He will not change! We know that changes will come in our everyday lives. Change is hard for many of us. Often we find ourselves struggling against change. Knowing that God is always here for us to turn to and He always has a plan makes dealing with change easier. He will not leave or forsake us. He will not change His mind about loving us. He will not change His mind about saving us. He will not change His mind about providing for us. He will not change!

Lord, how much this verse means to us as we live our lives in a changing world. When we face change at every corner You've given us such a wonderful promise that You will never change. Thank You for Your steadfastness in our lives.

BELOVED

3 John 1:2

Beloved, I wish above all things that thou mayest prosper
and be in health, even as thy soul prospereth.

Are you battling a disease? Are you coping with an ongoing illness? No matter what illness may attack our bodies there is no illness that can touch the soul that belongs to Christ. This verse tells us that God wishes for us to prosper in our health. Notice that He calls us beloved. He's speaking to us, His beloved children, encouraging us. He wishes for us good health in our earthly bodies just as our soul prospers when we trust in God. He saves our souls and He holds us eternally in His hands. Every part of us.

Father, I'm so thankful that no matter what is going on in my life that You are ultimately in control. You are my Creator and You know my days. Help me to give them back to You Lord for Your glory.

SUPPLY

Psalm 37:4

Delight thyself also in the LORD; and he shall give thee the desires of thine heart.

When you were a kid did you have something that you really wanted? Maybe it was a new bike or new baby doll. Perhaps it was a new baby brother or sister. You actually may have prayed for those things. Wasn't it easy to trust God with our requests when we were young and innocent? We didn't think twice about asking God for anything. I wonder why that changed as we got older. You might say it's because we knew what to pray for. Really? Because my belief is that God wants us to bring all of our desires to him. It's actually scripturally correct to ask God for our desires. Don't you want to be childlike with God and just be open and honest with him about your needs and wants? This verse doesn't tell us that there is a limit to what we should pray for. It tells us that we should be careful for nothing but always in all things lay our request before God.

God help us to be thankful for all that we have and to look to You to supply our needs.

Anxiety

Matthew 6:34

"Take therefore no thought for the morrow: for the morrow shall take thought for things of itself. Sufficient unto the day is the evil thereof."

Anxiety is something we hear a lot about in today's world. We are given medicines, exercises, and therapy to aid in the battle against anxiety. Anxiety can destroy us physically, emotionally and mentally. Where do we find peace from our worries? Is there an answer for the strife we feel around us? How do we not worry about tomorrow? I've found in my Christian walk that it takes a lot of faith not to worry. Not to worry about the bills, our futures, our children, our parents and the list goes on and on. God tells us in His word that we shouldn't worry about tomorrow. That sounds simple enough doesn't it? I believe the more we practice not worrying the easier it becomes for us to give our fears to God. Isn't that what anxiety really is? A fear of bad things happening. God gave us His word that He would take care of us today. He's saying in this verse that we should live today. Let Him take care of what happens today and tomorrow.

Lord, we ask that today You give us a break from our fears and let us realize that You are bigger than any fear that we may have. Help us each morning to give You back that day so that You can work in us. We thank You for being the same today, tomorrow and always.

HEARING

Isaiah 65:24

And it shall come to pass, that before they call, I will answer; and while they are yet speaking, I will hear.

Often times in my prayer life, I shoot off a quick prayer to God for this need or that need. Sometimes, it's something personal but sometimes it's for the needs of others. It may be for a situation that I have just learned about. It may be about something that has just happened. I make it a practice when I hear an ambulance to stop for a second and say a prayer for whoever it's going to. These are moment to moment prayers I guess you could say. On a regular, almost daily basis, I get on my knees before God. Usually, it's just for a short few minutes. I try to use these times to acknowledge who God is in my life. I use this time to pray for specific needs. Then there are those times with my heart heavy and breaking that I fall on my knees begging God for divine intervention in situations. These are the times that I am broken before God. These are the times that I call on Him, my Abba Daddy God. I still remember as a child running to my earthly daddy when things were too big for me to handle. I will always remember the love in his hands when he took mine. My dad tried to make things better for me and he almost always did. I'm so thankful that this verse in Isaiah assures us that our Heavenly Father is there for us. He already knows our petitions even before we call! He tells us that even as we are laying our prayers before Him that he is hearing us. What sweet peace to know that He loves us that much.

Lord, we come to You today acknowledging who You are in our lives. We thank You God for Your tender mercies. We thank You God for hearing and answering our prayers. We thank You for being our Abba Daddy God.

Control

Isaiah 32:18

And my people shall dwell in a peaceable habitation, and in sure dwellings, and in quiet resting places;

This is a promise from our Heavenly father! Now I know that you may be thinking not in this world. There is too much hate and anger and wrongdoing for there to be peace. You can find peace though in the arms of our Father and in the promise of His word. When the world spins out of control and you can't seem to stop long enough to even get a grip on things, just breath a prayer to your Creator. He will show you a place to find peace and rest.

Lord, as we go about our lives today, we see so much that troubles us, things that we have no control over and things that we've lost control of. We ask You God to please take hold of these things and make a way for us.

Afraid

Psalm 27:1

The Lord is my light and my salvation; whom shall I fear? the Lord is the strength of my life; of whom shall I be afraid?

We don't have to be afraid. We don't have to worry about the darkness in this world. We don't have to live our lives in our own strength. We can rely on God to be our light, our Savior and our strength. Even when our world seems upside down and we don't see how we can go forward, we don't have to fear! We can rely on God to allay all of our fears. When I find myself afraid I reflect on scriptures such as this one. I find peace in God's promise of protection. He is the one that will protect me and calm all of my fears. Do you need to find peace in the middle of your storm? Are you trying to hang on as the wind rages around you? When your fears are bigger than you are, get into God's word. Start looking for promises in His word that will sustain you. The Lord is my light, whom shall I fear?

God, we have so many fears in this world. Remind us God that when we have Your light that there is no darkness that can consume us. Help us to seek You and give You all of our fears.

CHOOSE

Joshua 24:15

And if it seem evil unto you to serve the LORD, choose you this day whom ye will serve; whether the gods which your fathers served that [were] on the other side of the flood, or the gods of the Amorites, in whose land ye dwell: but as for me and my house, we will serve the LORD.

There is that word that makes all the difference in a person's life. The word *choose*. God gave us a commandment to choose whom we would serve, but He ultimately gave us the choice. I recently had a friend that questioned me on why God allowed us to have free will. He stated that it would be so much easier to serve God if you didn't have a choice. By that he was saying that if we didn't have to make a choice between right and wrong and God chose for us to only do right then we would always be in God's will. I've pondered that a lot since our conversation and I can see where he's coming from, however, God wanted us to choose to serve Him out of love for Him. He didn't want to force us to walk in His way because we had to. True, it seems it would be easier to have our minds made up for us, but that wasn't and isn't God's plan. It's up to us to choose whom we will serve.

God, thank You for allowing us to have a mind of our own. Thank You for giving us the ability to think and feel and love. Draw our hearts toward You so that we might choose wisely.

Words

Proverbs 15:1

A soft answer turneth away wrath: but grievous words stir up anger.

Many times I've responded in anger to a situation, I tend to just react before I give it any thought. Just this morning something happened that made me angry. I fumed and fumed inside my head about it. Then I gave it to God. Notice that I didn't give it to God to begin with, oh no, I spent time letting it grow bigger than it actually was. Then this small little voice came to me. It basically was saying something that you and I already know is true. I needed to take the high road, not to show my anger but instead stand firm in my Christian walk; yes, even when I'm angry, maybe especially when I'm angry. We could pour out words of anger and hate, and hurt our witness so much in moments like this. I'm still learning to be slow to anger and when anger takes hold of me to let it go quickly. I know it is one area in me God is still working on.

Father, please help me in this area, You know my heart, Lord, and You know how quickly I can get angry. Let me stop and think before I react.

ACTION

I John 3:18

My little children let us not love in word, neither in tongue; but in deed and truth.

Have you ever heard the saying "lip service"? I believe that we try to express our love with lip service. It's easy to say I love you, I love my family, and I love people. Do we? Love is action, in deeds and in truth. Do you show it? It's time together, a smile, a hug, a shoulder, a prayer. It's taking time. Think about how much Christ loved us and what He did to show it. Few of us, if any will ever be asked to lay down our life to show our love. Jesus did in deed and in truth! Show some love today!

Lord help us to express our love for each other more often and in better ways. Remind us that a smile or a hug goes a long way when someone needs it. Thank You for showing us Your love by sending us Your son.

SHEEP

Psalm 23:1

The Lord is my shepherd; I shall not want.

When I think about shepherds of course I think about the shepherds in the Bible. I think about how the shepherd would lay down his life to protect one of his sheep. The shepherd was the ultimate protector for his flock. He would leave them all to go search and rescue one lost sheep. Are you one of God's sheep? Is He your Shepherd? Are you allowing Him to provide for you? He will be your protector and your provider. He will save your soul and give you a home in heaven! Have you left the fold? You see God doesn't leave you. He doesn't stop being your Shepherd. We move from God. If you've moved away from God and you need Him to leave the ninety nine and come for you, just ask! He will reach down and grab you by the hand and pull you back into the fold and give you redemption. He loves His sheep! Ask God to count you as one of His sheep today!

Father God, I need You to be my Shepherd; I'm tired of feeling lost and frightened. I need You to reach down and bring me back to Your fold. Thank You for accepting me as I am and loving me.

BROKENHEARTED

Psalm 34:18

The Lord is close to the brokenhearted, he rescues those whose spirits are crushed.

I seem to be led over and over to verses that bring hope and comfort. Some of you may be in that place right now, the place that you could use just a glimpse of hope, feel a blanket of comfort or feel your load getting lighter. It seems on a daily basis we or people around us experience so much heartache, so much brokenness. It often feels like our spirits are being crushed. Whether by tragedy in our lives, or an illness or someone we trust hurting us. We often feel beat down and like a failure. We get to the point in our lives that we aren't sure where to turn. We may wonder if there is a light at the end of the tunnel. Is there calm after the storm? When will the hurting be over? We may have to wade, push and cry our way through the pain, but we are not without hope and we are not without comfort. Our Lord is our Hope and our Comforter. Let Him lighten your load today!

Lord, We come to You today asking You to wrap us in Your loving arms! Let Your words fill our spirits and give us comfort and hope for tomorrow.

Burdens

Psalm 55:22

Cast thy burden upon the Lord, and he shall sustain thee:
he shall never suffer the righteous to the Lord.

Cast! If you know anything about fishing, you know that you throw your line into the water to catch a fish. You know that you throw your nets in the water to catch multiple fish at one time. The meaning of cast is to throw something forcefully in a specified direction. So this verse is telling us to throw our burdens on the Lord! How freeing is that? I can just visualize throwing them, just turning loose of them and giving them one big heave at my Heavenly Father. He can handle all of our burdens. None of them are too big or too hard for Him to handle. He may choose to walk beside us as we carry that burden, or He may choose to carry us while we carry it, or He may choose to take it away completely so that we are no longer burdened with it. Today throw your burdens and your cares on the Lord! He's got this!

Lord God, today I ask that You remind us that You are our Creator and that You know all things. I pray God that You will catch our burdens and cares as we let go of them and fling them at Your feet. I pray that You will give us peace and hope and that You truly will sustain us.

Distress

II Samuel 22:7

In my distress I called upon the Lord, and cried to my God: and he did hear my voice out of his temple, and my cry did enter into his ears.

How often when things are going well do we call upon the Lord? Some of us call on Him daily, seeking direction for the day or rest for the night. However, when bad things happen and we find no other avenue for solace, or in other words in our distress, we call upon the Lord. According to this verse we aren't the only ones that do that! Even in biblical times, people called out to the Lord in their distress. They cried to the Lord. Many times in my life I've found myself on my knees in humble contrition crying out to my Father. In my distress I've begged Him to heal hurts, heal hearts, forgive sins, and heal human bodies, and so on. This verse says He did hear my voice! Oh what sweet peace, my Father heard my voice. He rendered His ear and listened to my pleas. Sometimes, I wouldn't have immediate answers to my prayer, but I did have an immediate sense that my Father heard me. Then it is my place to wait for Him to show me the next step. Are you distressed today? Do you have a problem that you can't fix? Do you have a need? Cry out to the Lord in your distress!

Lord, I pray right now that You will reassure us that You listen to Your children's prayers. I pray God that You will let our cries enter Your ears. Thank You Father God that You care about us and our needs.

Filled with Joy

Isaiah 55:12

For ye shall go out with joy, and be led forth with peace: the mountains and the hills shall break forth into singing, and all the trees of the field shall clap their hands.

Joy. Have you ever known someone that you thought was full of joy? How would you describe that person? Maybe you would say, "They always have a smile on their face, or maybe they always have a kind word to say." Sometimes can't you just see it in their eyes? It's a presence about them, a peace you can see and feel. Do you ever wonder what makes them joyous? This verse is about joy! Pure joy oozing out of even God's creations! Can you imagine the mountains and hills singing with joy? What a sound that would be! Think about the trees clapping their hands with joy! Just think about going out in joy and being led forth with peace! What a difference that would and could make in the lives of people we meet. Today as you face a new day, look out to the hills and imagine them singing! Look out to the trees and imagine you can hear them clapping for joy, and then interact with them and let yourself be filled with joy! Find joy in something simple today!

Father, we thank You that You created us in Your likeness. Lord, we are so blessed with Your beautiful creation. The mountains and the trees and the oceans. We thank You that we have so much to be joyful for. Help us Lord, to share the reason for our joy today.

Deliverance

Exodus 14:13

And Moses said unto the people, Fear ye not, stand still, and see the salvation of the Lord, which he will shew to you today, for the Egyptians whom ye have seen today ye shall see them no more forever.

Can we say deliverance? Wow! God told Moses right here in this verse that He was delivering His people from the Egyptians! God tells Moses to watch (stand still) and watch what He is about to do! The Lord was about to take care of the Egyptians once and for all and Moses would never hear from them again! How amazing that must have been for Moses to hear! Today, we need deliverance from all types of things. Granted, sometimes it may still be a person or a group of people that has a stronghold on us or still trying to oppress us. It may be a sickness or a drug or alcohol problem, an abusive or inappropriate relationship. As individuals we may feel trapped or oppressed by various things in our lives. Whatever it is that you need deliverance from today, do like Moses did and ask God! Then watch God show up and show out! Don't you love the attitude of God in this verse? He's reassuring His child Moses, telling him not to fear and to be on the watch because He is about to take care of business on Moses' behalf. God can take care of business on your behalf too! Just stand still and watch!

Lord today, there is so much in this world that oppresses us and that we get bogged down in. I pray God that You will continue to hear the prayers of Your children, just as You heard Moses' prayer. I pray that You will give swift deliverance from the things in this world that are consuming Your children. Thank You God for divine intervention on our behalf!

Tranquility

Isaiah 26:3

Thou wilt keep him in perfect peace, whose mind is stayed on thee: because he trusteth in thee.

Now more than ever I believe that we are looking for peace. When asking a group of people in a social setting what they would like to see in this world the most, you would probably have several answers of peace. World peace, inner peace, and peace about decisions they need to make. I think about all the times that the word peace is used in the Bible. The word peace is mentioned 426 times in God's word. The definition of peace is *freedom from disturbance or quiet and tranquility*. Sometimes, after getting home from work, I love to sit down in my home with no sound and no lights. I enjoy being able to have total quiet and no disturbances for a little while. This particular verse tells us that God will give us peace if we keep our mind focused on Him. I think this means peace in a true sense of the word. If we will let our minds and hearts focus on Him, then other things become unimportant. Our problems diminish when we seek the peace of God. Today I pray that you will find peace for whatever it is you have in your life that troubles you.

Lord, I pray that You will let Your peace prevail in our lives. I pray You will woo us to You to give You our problems. I pray You will place people in our lives to help us when we need it the most. Thank You for Your peace that is above and beyond anything that this world can offer.

Given

Luke 2:21

And when eight days were accomplished for the circumcising of the child, his name was called JESUS, which was so named of the angel before he was conceived in the womb.

Do you know my Jesus? Do you know Him as your Savior? Today as we rush to one another's homes carrying carefully wrapped gifts for our loved ones, let us go back in time. Over 2000 years ago God gave us the most important and precious gift that we will ever receive! Jesus! Then God in His infinite wisdom gave us the opportunity and the power (Romans 1:16) to share the story of Jesus. To go tell it on the mountain that Jesus Christ is born! What are you going to do with Jesus this Christmas? Are you going to worship Him as the King of Kings? Are you going to be so busy giving and receiving material things that you leave him by the wayside? Whether you are assembling together as a church body or gathering with your friends and families in your homes, STOP for a few minutes to reflect; to savor and to worship my Jesus! If you don't know my Jesus there is no better time on earth to search for Him just as the shepherds and wise men did. They found Him then and you can find Him now.

God thank You for allowing us to still find You! Keep us focused on the true meaning of the holidays.

NEW CREATION

II Corinthians 5:17

Therefore if any man be in Christ, he is a new creature: old things are passed away; behold, all things are become new.

This morning on the way to work, I noticed a sign that stated "new creations salon coming soon." I thought about the church that is being built right down the road from my home "New Beginnings." It made me stop and think. I believe in today's world we are constantly looking for something new. Why do think that is? Why is it that we always seem to need something more, bigger, greater, better, newer? In comparison to what the Bible teaches us about being new what else could or should we want? We are new creatures in Christ. Therefore, we lack nothing; there is nothing that the heavenly Father can't provide for us. Still, we toil, work and weasel to get more. We seem to have the need to constantly reinvent ourselves. Christ is the only one that enables us to be reinvented, it is though Him. That is the most important new beginning that you could ever experience. To experience a new birth in Him, a new joy in Him, a new love in Him. Are you ready for a new beginning?

Thank You God that You gave me a brand new beginning! Thank You God that You walk with me each day and provide for me.

Doubt

James 1:6

But let him ask in faith, nothing wavering. For he that wavereth is like a wave of the sea driven with the wind and tossed.

Sometimes, in life we probably feel like a leaf being blown by the wind. We need to realize that no matter where the winds of life may be blowing us we can find stability in the Lord! That stability comes by having faith in God and believing in His word. I'm unsure why we have trouble putting our problems before God in total faith. When we sit in a chair we have full faith that the chair will hold us up. We don't give it one thought before we plop down. That is the kind of faith we must have in order to see what God can really do in our lives! Today is a great day to put your faith in God and give Him all of your cares and concerns without giving it a single thought. No doubting, just having faith!

Lord, today we thank You that You are able and willing to accept our problems and our burdens. We are thankful that You remind us in Your word to trust without doubt. Thank You for loving us and giving us hope.

WORRY

Isaiah 57:2

He shall enter into peace: they shall rest in their beds,
[each one] walking [in] his uprightness.

Sweet, wonderful peace. What would you do to find it and what would you pay to have it? The kind of peace that takes away your worries. The kind that encompasses your cares. No worries to take to bed with you at night and none to wake up to in the morning. That is the peace that my Father can give us! He offers us a chance to enter into his peace. We won't need any other kind, because his is the best. Our problems won't necessarily go away when we accept our Father's peace, but they will seem so much smaller and more manageable. He assures us that if we place our trust in Him we can and will have this peace.

Lord, I pray that You will remind us of how much You love us and how You want what is best for us at all times. Help us to trust You with everything in our lives, big and small and lay us down to sleep in perfect peace knowing that You are in control.

Creator

Isaiah 45:12

I made the earth and all the people living on it. With my own hands I stretched out the skies, and I commanded all the armies in the sky.

He's got the whole world in His hands! He does, you know? After all, He created it so it's His. We so often forget that don't we? That He created it first and then created us to take care of it. That He gave us this world that we are living in. What a big responsibility that was and how much He must have trusted in us to give us that responsibility. Do you take that responsibility seriously? It should be our pleasure to get up and enjoy each new day and eagerly take on whatever task He puts before us for that day. What in His beautiful world have you taken special notice of lately? Have you stopped to appreciate the beauty of this world? I know there is a lot in this world that is bad, but that's because man turned from God and spoiled His original plan. But He redeemed us and now He gives us so many beautiful things and blessings to enjoy. Don't miss out on the simple blessings that a new day can bring.

Thank You God for creating such a beautiful place for us to live! Thank You for the sunrise and the sunsets. Help us to never take it for granted.

PROMISES

Isaiah 55:8

For my thoughts are not your thoughts, neither are your ways my ways, saith the LORD.

When my mom had a stroke after a moderately simple surgery I learned what this verse really meant. I had six and a half weeks with my mom before God took her home. I sat by her bed for eleven straight days while she was in a coma. When she woke up on that eleventh day, she couldn't speak at all; she couldn't move her right side very much and there wasn't a lot of recognition for us in her eyes. The day she reached up and stroked my daughter's hair with recognition in her eyes will be indelibility written on my heart. As she started to improve, we felt sure that she was going to recover and come home. She was being prepared to move to therapy when she had a big setback. Falling on my face before God I begged Him not to take my momma. I read scriptures and I cried and I prayed some more and I waited on Him to act. He did act; He left her with us for those six and half weeks so that I could adjust to the idea of her homegoing. My pastor came to the hospital many times and he kept telling me that he could see the peace of God in me. Oddly enough, I felt that peace too even when things were the bleakest. I never gave up waiting and believing that God could heal her and bring her home, but I had to accept that His ways are on not our ways and that He knew best. It's been seven long years since I held my momma's hand, but I have a promise from God that I WILL see her again. I thank God for time to let go, to mourn and to accept His will.

Lord, help us to remember at all times that You know best even when it's so hard to accept. We must remember God that all of Your plans are perfect. Thank You God that I have hope in You that I will see my loved ones again.

Sleep

Psalm 4:8

I will both lay me down in peace, and sleep: for thou, LORD, only makest me dwell in safety.

When you were a child did your mom and dad tuck you in and read you a bedtime story? Maybe, they came in to say goodnight and join you in your goodnight prayers. They were making sure that you were ready for a good night's sleep. They were giving you assurances that they were right there and would be there in the morning. This is such a sweet promise from our Heavenly Father. What a great way to end our day! Knowing that when we lay our head down to rest that our Father will be there. Think of it like God reading you a bedtime story with this verse. Jesus assures us that He will allow us a good night's sleep because we trust in Him and His plan is to take care of us, just like our parents took care of us when we were small.

Thank You God for Your promise of rest.

RESCUED

Matthew 14:30

But when he saw the wind boisterous, he was afraid; and beginning to sink, he cried, saying, Lord, save me.

We all know this story of Peter walking on the water to meet Jesus in the midst of a storm. If you read the two verses prior to this one you will see something miraculous. You will see that as long as Peter had his eyes on Jesus he was indeed walking on water! He wasn't afraid of sinking because his mind was set on Jesus. Don't you think that is what happens to us so much of the time? We get our minds set on God and we begin our journey and things are going along smoothly and then, *wham*! We see the churning seas out in front of us and we lose our focus! As soon as we lose our focus and take our eyes off of the Lord, we begin to sink. Maybe not physically but spiritually. Jesus did not let Peter drown in the boisterous sea and He will not allow you to drown either. Jesus reached down and grabbed Peter by the hand and brought him back to safety. That's what our God does for us, He reaches down at the very moment that our storms are the wildest. He pulls us back to safety and He calms the storms. Want you let God pull you up out of your storms today?

God, we are so amazed by Your wonderful love for us. Especially when we lose our focus and begin to flounder. Thank You for picking us up and putting our feet back on dry ground.

CONTROL

James 3:8

But the tongue can no man tame; it is an unruly evil, full of deadly poison.

Take special notice to the words "no man" in this verse. As many times as I've read and heard this verse spoken about the tongue, I don't think I ever took note of those two very important words. NO MAN can tame the tongue, but that doesn't mean that it can't be tamed! It means that we must give our tongues over to the Lord. He created our tongues when He created us so it is His anyway. I know that's a strange thought but true. If you have ever tried to control your tongue on your own you know that it is difficult to say the least. Now you may say, I don't curse or speak profanities, but it's not just those types of things that causes hurt. Have you ever gossiped? Have you ever lashed out before you thought? I would venture to say that we all have done these things. It's just that we don't think about it as sin. Today give some thought to your tongue. Think before you speak about anything. Let God control this important part of you!

Father, I pray that in the mornings as we prepare to go about our days that we ask that You control our tongues. I pray that we might use it to praise You and to share Your love instead of hurting and destroying.

SHARING

Luke 8:39

Return to thine own house, and shew how great things God hath done unto thee. And he went his way, and published throughout the whole city how great things Jesus had done unto him.

Let's not forget to praise God when he does something for us. Many times in church or Sunday school, we have prayer request and needs that we take to the Father. It seems the list goes on and more and more people are sick, dying, brokenhearted and jobless. Every so often we will have someone give a praise report for an answered prayer. I think we need to do a lot more of giving God thanks and praise for the many things that He has done for us. We need to stop and thank Him for the little things as well. I often thank God for a good parking place or getting on a busy road without incident. He's in control of these things too. When was the last time that you spent your entire prayer time thanking God? When was the last time that you shouted out your window what God is doing in your life? We need to be busy sharing with the world that we serve a God that loves us and answers our prayers! We need to proclaim His greatness throughout the whole city!

Lord, we fail so many times to stop and say thank You for answered prayers, but we fail even more when we don't share the news of Your greatness with others. Helps us Lord to be bolder in sharing Your awesomeness!

Provision

Luke 12:24

Consider the ravens: for they neither sow nor reap; which neither have storehouse nor barn; and God feedeth them: how much more are ye better than the fowls?

Isn't this the most amazing promise? God is promising of us right here that He will take care of us! How I wish that we could truly grab hold of this and take it to heart. Oh, I know you might say, "I believe it." Do you really? He's reminding us that He takes care of those He created. He created us in His own image so why shouldn't He care for us more than the birds or any of his other creation? Once, years ago in my earlier Christian years, I just couldn't see how we financially would make ends meet that month. So I prayed. I prayed that God would give me a sign. Just something that I could grab onto and take to heart. That afternoon I went to the mailbox and there was my answer. It was a $7.00 rebate check from something that I didn't even remember sending in. You see God knew before I ever prayed that prayer that I was going to need some assurance on that day. He had the answer to my prayer on the way before I even prayed it! That's just how our God is! He promised us he would take care of us and He never breaks a promise. When you feel like your storehouse is empty or there isn't going to be enough food for your family, just pray. God has already taken care of the need.

Lord, I am so thankful that You hear our cries and that answer when we need it the most. Thank You for revealing Your plan to me!

BIGGER

Psalm 8:3-5

When I consider your heavens, the work of your fingers, The moon and the stars, which you have ordained; What is man that You take thought of him, And the son of man that You care for him?

At times when something out of my control is going on in my life, I almost chant the words "My God is bigger." They become my mental mantra. Why? For the reassurance it gives me. We are his children; He loved us so much He sent His son to die for us. Why wouldn't He want what is best for us? He is in control at all times, even when we aren't. I find it interesting that when I relinquish control to Him in a given situation suddenly it doesn't seem big at all. Not in comparison to Who is taking care of it for me. Is your God bigger than anything going on in your life? The answer is beyond a doubt YES!

Praise the Lord! My God is so much bigger than I can begin to believe or understand! Thank You God for being my great big God!

Sufficient

Exodus 3:14

And God said unto Moses, I AM THAT I AM: and he said, Thus shalt thou say unto the children of Israel, I AM hath sent me unto you.

Who do you say God is? If you are like me, God fills many places in your heart so He bears many names as well. We know in the Bible that God was called by different names in different languages. Ehyeh Asher Ehyeh is one that I had not heard until I began studying some of God's names. It means the eternal, all sufficient God. Wow! That should just about sum up any name that we could possibly need to attach to our God! He is eternal and we know that He is all sufficient. It is the name that is used in reference to this verse in Exodus. I cannot begin to image how Moses felt when God gave him this verse. God wanted Moses to let the people of Israel know that HE was GOD! He wanted them to know that He was sending Moses to them as their leader. In biblical times, I think it would have been easier to believe it if a man walked up to you and said "I AM sent me", but maybe not. After all God wasn't visible to them either. I only know that God was, is and always will be the great I AM!

Lord, how humbling it is to think of the many places in our lives that You fill. How magnificent is Your name!

Near

Jeremiah 23:23

Am I a God at hand, saith the Lord, and not a God afar off?

Where is our God? When I was a child we lived in the country. There was a pretty little creek that ran down below our house. We kids would go down there and spend hours at a time looking for salamanders and crickets and so on. I was never afraid to wander around on our acre of land because I knew my parents were at home. They were at my home base keeping an eye and ear tuned to my whereabouts. They always knew where I was. That is how our God is. He is in our Heavenly home keeping a watch over us as we go about our days. He is not far off from us but He is paying attention to where we are. He knows what His children are doing. We cannot venture anywhere that He is not able to see and hear us. He is here right now with us each day and everywhere.

Thank You God for being our Elohei Mikkarov, God who is near. We can't begin to fathom the love that You have for Your children. Thank You for that love!

Banner

Exodus 17:15

And Moses built an altar, and called the name of it Jehovah-nissi.

I've always thought about God's love as a blanket. I guess it's the idea of a blanket wrapping around me, warming and protecting me from whatever is outside of it. Jehovah-nissi, the Lord is my banner. I find in Exodus that God described himself as a banner. In my mind this is like the blanket idea. While the children of Israel were on their journey after they left Egypt there was a battle. The people of Israel won that battle and God told Moses to write it down that He was Jehovah-nissi. He did this because He wanted to make sure when Joshua took over from Moses he would have a reminder of God's faithfulness in battle. This battle was a symbol of the battles that would be fought by Christians through the years. Not just physical battles but all kinds of battles that we fight in our daily lives. God is still our banner and our Victor when we rely on Him to fight our battles. There is no battle that is too big for God to win. No matter what battle you are fighting right now you can call on Jehovah-nissi for the win. When you are going through a battle just remember that we will always have battles but the important thing is that God will always be the winner!

Father God, I am so thankful for Your many names in the Bible. I'm thankful that You gave us those names to remind us of the different ways that You take care of us. Let us always remember to give You our battles.

Security

Hebrews 11:10

For he looked for a city which hath foundations, whose builder and maker is God.

God promises us a Heavenly home in the scriptures. I can't begin to imagine how perfect it is going to be! As I write this a sweet woman of God has just been called home. She is walking in that city Whose maker is God! I imagine that she received a great big hug from her husband when she entered the city. She is reunited with all of her loved one's and will be eternally happy! The scripture tells me that we will have no worries, or pain. We won't face depression or crime or hate or death any longer. What a place Heaven must be! There is no need for light because Jesus is the light. We will be wholly God's and reign with Him forever!

Thank You Jesus for securing our home in Heaven! I can't begin to think how perfect it's going to be but I know it will be because You've told me so.

DEFEATED

Matthew 4:10

Then saith Jesus unto him, Get thee hence, Satan: for it is written, Thou shalt worship the Lord thy God, and him only shalt thou serve.

The Lord said it and he meant it! I have heard people say "get behind me Satan" for years, but right here we find it's biblical. Jesus told the devil to get away from Him. That is just what we need to be doing too. Think about how much easier it would be to face each day knowing that the devil has been defeated. You can claim this as one of God's promises! You can give God complete control over your life because He has defeated the enemy! We are to worship our Creator, the one true God. We shall not succumb to the devil's devises, he has no control over us when we commit to serving God. Will we still have to do battle with the devil? Yes, as a matter of fact, the stronger your commitment to God, the more the devil will hound you. We must remember who the victory goes to in the ultimate battle. We already know the end of the story and we will not just persevere but we will be victorious! We will have victory in Jesus!

Father, I'm so thankful and amazed that You stand in the gap for me on a daily basis. You have defeated the enemy once and for all and because of that I will be with You in glory one day.

Speaking

Isaiah 55:11

So shall My word be which goes forth from My mouth; it shall not return to Me empty, without accomplishing what I desire, and without succeeding in the matter for which I sent it.

Do you remember the old commercial about E.F. Hutton? It went along the lines of, "When E.F. Hutton speaks, people listen". I think about this commercial when I think about people listening to Jesus. In biblical times when Jesus spoke people listened. Some of those that listened didn't like what He was saying, however, some who listened had their lives dramatically changed. We know that when Jesus spoke thing happened! According to scripture when Jesus spoke the mute could speak, the blind could see and the lame could walk. Jesus calmed the mighty winds and raised the dead. Are we listening to Jesus as He speaks to us today? We know that He still calms the winds and heals the sick. It's our job as a Christian to keep listening and staying tuned to His voice. Keep listening, God is still speaking!

Lord, thank You so much for Your words, we thank You for Your healing power and for Your direction in our lives.

THE CROSS

I Peter 3:15

But sanctify the Lord God in your hearts: and be ready always to give an answer to every man that asketh you a reason of the hope that is in you with meekness and fear:

Years ago I received a cross necklace as a gift. I wore it every day no matter what other jewelry I wore. One day a salesman came by my office, He asked me why I wore the cross. I took the opportunity to tell him why I wore it and where my faith and hope was established. Wearing that cross was a reminder to me of what my Savior did for me on the cross. It was an outward sign of an inward conversion. You may not choose to wear something that is indicative of your Christian faith, but for me it was a way to open up doors to share the gospel. Whether we wear a symbol of God's love or not, we should always be willing and ready to tell others what He means in our life.

Father, thank You for the cross that You bore for me, thank You that I don't have to wear a symbol of Your love for it to apply to me. Thank You for the opportunity to share Your love with others.

AGAPE

I John 4:19

We love Him because He first loved us.

That's amazing to me in itself HE loved us! He loves us! He will always love us! HE wants HIS children to have the desires of their hearts. HE wants HIS children to come before Him boldly leaving their burdens, their needs, and their desires at HIS feet! Why is it so hard for His children to understand that? He will never leave or forsake us. Every day I fall so short in serving HIM but I am more than thankful that He is a forgiving, merciful, loving Savior. He is a Friend, Confidante, Deliverer, and my Abba Daddy God. We should be overwhelmed with love for Him in return.

Lord, where would we be without Your love and mercy? Thank You so much for loving us!

ANGELS

Hebrews 13:2

Be not forgetful to entertain strangers: for thereby some have entertained angels unawares.

Years ago on a summer day there was a knock at my door. I went to the door and there was a lady standing there that I did not know. She stated that she and some others were down the road clearing off some land. Now, you have to understand that I live in a rural area in a small town. We usually know everything that is happening around us, so I was a little surprised by this. She then proceeded to ask if I could give her a glass of water. I didn't invite her in but I did go to the kitchen and get a large plastic cup and fill it with ice and water. She took the cup and left. I never saw her again and never saw any evidence of land clearing in our area. After she was gone, I reflected on the Bible verse about entertaining angels unaware. I've always wondered if I had just been visited by one of God's angels.

Lord, thank You for sending people our way that have needs that we can help with. Make us aware that we need to always be willing to do what we can to help others.

HOLY

Leviticus 10:10

And that ye may put difference between holy and unholy, and between unclean and clean;

Do we know what is holy and clean anymore? Are we allowing the lines between the two to become blurred? I know that we are bombarded by unholy things every day. It seems that we aren't as shocked by evil as we should be. Every day we become a little more desensitized with the evil infiltrating our world. When we begin to think its okay to watch an R rated movie or read a sketchy book, then we have become insensitive to what is holy. I don't think we start out to allow uncleanliness in our lives, I believe it sneaks up on us. We hear others talking about a movie or a book or a behavior and we think if they think it's okay then it must be. This is the devil doing what the devil does best, throwing us off the path that we need to be on for Jesus. I think we have to be careful not to fall into the acceptance trap that the world so readily offers us. We need to know the difference in holy and unholy. We need to seek God's ways for our lives. Sometimes, we have to make a stand or at least walk away from those things that we know are unholy and unclean.

Father, help us as Your children to not fall into Satan's trap of sin and accepting things that are unholy and unclean. Help us to seek Your way in our lives.

Forgiveness

Luke 6:29

And unto him that smiteth thee on the one cheek offer also the other; and him that taketh away thy cloak forbid not to take thy coat also.

We've always heard the phrase "turn the other cheek" and we can assume that it came from this verse. It seems this verse is alluding to being physically slapped or stolen from; however, I believe that it can be emotionally done as well. Do you have someone in your life that you feel enjoys throwing out insults or placing you in the line of fire? I find in my life that there are people who seem to be really good at throwing me under the bus, so to speak. It's difficult to put this verse into effect when we have people in our lives that we feel are against us. I've had to learn that most of the time when someone is throwing out slanderous words against me, they are trying to make themselves look better for "some" reason. I think it's during these times that we must implement this verse in a very real way. We must pray that God will show us a way to love that person with His love. God loves us no matter what and He forgives ALL of our sins. Let us look to our Father for help in learning to turn the other cheek.

Lord, it's so hard to turn the other cheek when a person continues to hurt us, but we must remember that our actions hurt You at times to Lord. We know that You always forgive and allow redemption when we ask for it. Help us to show Your love to those who hurt us the most.

Thankful

Psalm 30:12

To the end that *my* glory may sing **praise** to You and not be silent. O Lord my **God**, I will give thanks to You forever.

Giving thanks should come easy for all of us. We have so much to be thankful for. When I was growing up my grandparents farmed. My grandparents worked hard and they shared what they had. I remember working hard right along with them in the fields picking okra that itched my arms and butter beans that hurt my back. I say all of this because it made me that much more thankful for the vegetables that we ate from that garden. God has been so gracious to us. He has given us eternal salvation from hell and so much more. I can't image my life without Christ. I am so blessed to call Him my Father and I am more thankful than words can ever express. I can't be silent when it comes to His love for me, nor do I want to be! He deserves all the honor and glory that we can give Him.

Father God, I'm so thankful that You loved me enough to save my soul from hell. I'm so thankful that You love me enough to care about everything that happens in my life.

Bought

I Corinthians 6:20

For ye are bought with a price: therefore glorify God in your body, and in your spirit, which are God's.

God paid a big price for us. The payment was His only son. We will never know this side of heaven why it had to be this way. God owns our bodies and our spirits. We should strive to glorify God by making the right decisions in our lives. We should keep our mind on Godly things and flood our spirit with Godly things. In order to keep our minds and bodies on Godly things, we have to purposefully thwart those things that are not of God. Sometimes, it's difficult to stay focused on the things of God when the world is throwing so much at us that is not godly. Some ways to keep ourselves from sinning is to stay in God's word, and gather with other Christians to edify each other and stay accountable along the journey.

Lord, words cannot express how grateful I am for Your son! I can't imagine the anguish that it must have caused You to see Your son die on the cross. Thank You for sacrificing Your best!

LONG SUFFERING

Psalm 86:15

But You, O Lord, are a God full of compassion, and gracious, Longsuffering and abundant in mercy and truth.

Compassion, grace and longsuffering. Wow! Those are three things that our world today needs a lot more of. Starting with myself. How about mercy and truth? I fail to show these traits in my life too many times. I need to be more conscientious about showing Christ love. I'm so thankful that God is compassionate and gracious to me. He is long-suffering when I sin again and again and have to go to Him for forgiveness. He doesn't make me feel worthless or insignificant. He just reaches down and picks me up, dusts me off and sets me on my way again, forgiven! When my heart is breaking and I can't seem to go forward, He renews my strength. In those moments that I have doubts, He gives me truth. He is an amazing God and I am humbled to call Him my Father!

Lord, thank You for the love that You give to me, a love that no human can possible extend. Thank You for holding on to me always and forever.

NEWNESS

Romans 8:10

And if Christ is in you, the body is dead because of sin, but the Spirit is life because of righteousness.

Only through God can we begin to have anything about us that is righteous. We have to ask Christ to live in us in order to have new life in Him. Sin is deadly and will destroy everything we have if and when we allow it to. Our earthly bodies will die one of these days, but our Christ filled spirit will live forever. We will always struggle with sin during our time on earth, but we have freedom from that sin in Christ. Isn't it awesome to think that one day we will be wholly pure and wholly His!

God, I thank You for forgiving my sins. I am so thankful to have Your forgiveness and love.

In The Beginning

Genesis 1:1

In the beginning God created the heaven and the earth.

You know how excited we are when we begin a new project. We are so excited to see how it turns out. Can you imagine how God must have felt as He began creating the world? I honestly can't imagine the awesomeness of the creation as it came into being. How amazing that our God SPOKE and the stars appeared! He gave us the light from the sun and the moon. He separated the water from the dry land and then He created all types of animals and birds and fish. He created a perfect world and chose to create man to live it in and take care of it for Him, the man Adam that we are all descendants of. Isn't that totally awesome that God had such a plan?

Thank You father God for creating this wonderful place that we know as earth.

Confession

James 5:16

Confess your trespasses to one another, and pray for one another, that you may be healed. The effective, fervent prayer of a righteous man avails much.

"You want me to tell others about my sins?" Yikes! That is just not something that most of us want to do. Most of us had rather keep our sins quiet and hidden. It's hard enough for us to admit to ourselves and to God that we have sinned. I have learned in my life that when I find myself in a situation that it helps to share it with a friend. Knowing that my friend can listen to my problems and not judge me is a huge relief. Also, knowing that my friend will not share my problems with anyone other than God is reassuring. How often have you gone to a friend with a prayer request? No matter how big the problem is it seems smaller when shared with a friend. So God really was onto something when He suggested that we share our sins with others and pray for one another. He knew way before we did that joys are doubled and sorrows divided when shared with a friend.

Thank You God for instructing us in how we can find earthly help for our transgressions. Thank You for knowing us to the extent that You know our every thought and deed. Thank You for praying friends.

POWER

I Corinthians 1:18

For the preaching of the cross is to them that perish foolishness; but unto us which are saved it is the power of God.

The power of the cross! The cross that our Savior hung on that gave us eternal life! We couldn't be called Christians if it had not been for Christ coming into this world. However, it wasn't just His coming that allowed us to enter into heaven and gain favor with God. It was the fact that He died on the cross for you and me, that His blood was shed as the blood of the Lamb. In biblical times we know that a blood sacrifice had to be made for a man's sins to be forgiven. Jesus had to be our blood sacrifice so that once and for all our sins would be forgiven! The idea of the cross may not mean much to those who don't believe that Jesus died there for us. However, for those of us who have been changed because of His death we know that we are eternally saved from hell because Jesus shed His blood that day.

Thank You God for the cross! Thank You that You loved us so much that You allowed Your son's blood to be shed for us.

Eternity

John 17:3

And this is life eternal, that they might know thee the only true God, and Jesus Christ, whom thou hast sent.

Practice spending time with God now because if you are a Christian you are going to be spending eternity with Him! We might as well get used to the idea of spending time with God. After all, we will have a lot more days up in heaven with Him than we will down here. Can you imagine what that is going to be like? Today, I attended the funeral of a fellow church member. The pastor was preaching her funeral and something he said struck a chord with me. He said, "If we give God our time, he will give us His eternity". Now I know we have to have a personal relationship with God to enter heaven, but there is so much more to being a Christian. We should spend time with our Father, because getting to know Him better on earth will prepare us for what we will experience once we get to heaven.

Father, what a wonderful thought! That we will be able to see Your face and worship at Your feet for eternity!

Lifted Up

Psalm 40:2

He brought me up also out of an horrible pit, out of the miry clay, and set my feet upon a rock, and established my goings.

When I was a little girl my mom, dad and I would go for Sunday afternoon drives. A lot of times we would find ourselves on clay roads. Now if you don't know anything about clay roads, they are very slippery when it rains. On one occasion we found ourselves in a deep ditch on one of those clay roads. We had to get someone to pull our car out of the ditch. He pulled us out of the ditch and made sure we were able to proceed on our outing. Sometimes in life we get ourselves into the ditch and need someone to pull us out. Isn't it reassuring that when we fall by the wayside our Father will lift us up and place us back on our feet and send us on our way?

Thank You, Father, for pulling me up out of the ditches I get myself in. Thank You for placing my feet on solid ground and sending me on my way again.

CHOSEN

II Thessalonians 2:13

But we should always give thanks to God for you, brethren beloved by the Lord, because God has chosen you from the beginning for salvation through sanctification by the Spirit and faith in the truth.

Do you remember when you were in school and it came time to play games on the playground? I was always the scrawny little girl that nobody wanted on their team. Granted, I wasn't the strongest or fastest kid on the block so I tried not to take it personally. Still, it did sting a bit when I was the last one standing and no one had chosen me. But like a lot of sad stories mine has a very happy ending! I have been chosen to be on God's team! Yes, He chose me personally, He called my name when I was 15 years old and saved me from hell. He chose me for the most important job that a person can have, to share the gospel of Jesus Christ! All of the times that I wasn't chosen for a team dims in comparison to the fact that I've been chosen by the Best for the best team there is!

Lord, I thank You for calling me by name and choosing me! I am so humbled that You love me enough to know me by name.

MISSING THE MARK

Romans 7:15

For that which I do I allow not: for what I would, that do I not; but what I hate, that do I.

I often pondered what this scripture meant, but as I sit in my room at the beach being anxious over a rash that is reappearing I think I get it! I've been participating in some of the devotions that the 6 ladies here have been doing in the mornings but I've been eager to get to the beach and enjoy the sand, surf and sun. I've prayed quick prayers to God in the mornings or late at night and have failed to take time to give to Him. I've missed the mark and now that I'm worried about the reoccurring rash I turn to Him. NOW my mind has time for Him and I'm not too eager to do other things, NOW I'm ready to rush to my Father's arms. Why is it that I have to be reminded over and over who is in control of me and my life. I don't intentionally push God aside when I'm busy with a project or on vacation, but I allow other things to get in the way of staying connected to Him. I like Paul in this verse hate when I allow other things to crowd my time with God. I want to serve Him first and foremost.

Father, Forgive me for falling short and not doing the things that I need to do. Help me to keep my focus on You and to always put You first!

Prepared

Isaiah 54:13

And all thy children shall be taught of the Lord; and great shall be the peace of thy children.

The lifelong question that we ask children as they are growing up is, "What do you want to be when you grow up?" I wonder why we never ask them what they think God wants them to be. We help our kids choose subjects in high school to prepare for college courses. We encourage them to study those subjects and make good grades so they can prepared for a position in the world. I wonder how many parents think about our child's future in terms of what God wants for them. Taking our children to church, praying with them and immersing them in God's word are ways we can build their belief in our Father. Can you imagine what strong Christians and disciples we could help grow if we taught them to seek God's will early on in life and seek it more diligently? I believe that we would be amazed! We would be helping to prepare our children for the greatest journey ever!

Father, even though my child is an adult, I pray that You will help me to be a Christian leader in her life.

BUCKET LIST

Colossians 1:10

That ye might walk worthy of the Lord unto all pleasing, being fruitful in every good work, and increasing in the knowledge of God;

What's on your bucket list? Most of us these days seem to have a bucket list. A list of things that we want to accomplish, see, or do before we die. If we looked at different people's bucket list, there would be a myriad of things on it. I wonder if any of those things would have anything to do with serving God. I heard a message preached on this awhile back. It made me think if I had a bucket list what it might look like, spiritually speaking. I would certainly want to be sure of my salvation, securing my place in heaven. No one wants to go to hell, even if they claim they don't want to be a Christian. I would hope that along the way I would want to be Christ's servant, proclaiming His word and trying to carry out what I believe He leads me to do. Each of us as a Christian has a job to do for God. Hopefully, I will have discovered that God gave me spiritual gifts and will be using those to His glory. Yes, you too have a spiritual gift. God equipped all Christians with one. It may take us trying our hand in several works before we discover it. Not your typical bucket list is it? Maybe it should be though. I believe that we should be more concerned with where we are going with God and where we end up than what we might accomplish for ourselves throughout this life.

God in Heaven, thank You for giving us breath and the opportunities to do so many things as we go through this life, help us to remember that what we do for You is the only thing that will be eternal.

DISCONNECTED

Jude 1:21

Keep yourselves in the love of God, looking for the mercy of our Lord Jesus Christ unto eternal life.

Today I unplugged my computer and the screen became dimmer. I suddenly realized that is just how it is when I am not fully connected with God! The light that God placed in me grows dimmer when I do not stay connected to its power source! Have you been overwhelmed, overburdened and feeling disconnected? Maybe your battery is low. Think about it! When we go without food our bodies grow weak and we become less productive. We must have the nutrients in food to keep our body functioning properly. Don't you see that our spiritual life must have nourishment to grow as well? It absolutely does! Staying connected to God is easy if we make it a priority. We need to set aside time each day to power up with God!

Lord, thank You for reminding me in order for me to grow in You, I must stay connected. Thank You for always being ready for me to turn to You and gain back my strength.

Separated

Romans 8:38-39

For I am persuaded, that neither death, nor life, nor angels, nor principalities, nor powers, nor things present, nor things to come, Nor height, nor depth, nor any other creature, shall be able to separate us from the love of God, which is in Christ Jesus our Lord.

I have this underlined in my Bible and I have notes written in the back of my Bible instructing my loved ones to have this read at my funeral. It's such a powerful verse to me, because it assures me that no matter what, as long as I am saved by God's grace, I will never be separated from Him. I want my loved one's to remember God's promise in this verse. I want it to become real to them just as it is real to me in my life. I will be eternally with my Savior when I leave this earth. Nothing on earth or anywhere else will be able to separate me from the God I have loved and served. We don't have to wait until our funeral to realize the truths in this verse. Claim it today for your very own!

God, thank You so much for putting this truth in Your word for us to hold onto when our world is upside down and we feel all alone.

Magnified

Psalm 70:4

Let all those that seek thee rejoice and be glad in thee: and let such as love thy salvation say continually, Let God be magnified.

Let God be magnified! Do we feel it in our hearts? Do we speak it in our words? Do we show it in our actions? Today as I search my own heart, I want to be bolder proclaiming God's love and what He has done and is doing in my life. I want to be a better servant, quick to volunteer when an opportunity comes open. I want to be a better witness, ready and willing to jump right in when the door opens. My desire is for people not to see me but to see the One who is living and working inside of me to make me what I am. Let God be magnified in your life today!

Lord how often we stand back and wait on someone else to take on the job that needs doing, or witness to someone. Help us God to be bold while we are about Your business and to seek ways to magnify Your Holy name!

COMFORT

Psalm 56:8

Thou tellest my wanderings: put thou my tears into thy bottle: *are they* not in thy book?

God knows all about us, He knows all the paths that life has taken us and He has been with us on each path. He has seen all of our tears and keeps account of them. In this verse David is reminding God of where he's been and the tears he's cried. He is reassured because God in His faithfulness to David has kept record, not of David's faults or wrong doings but of his pain and strife. When I think about this verse and how it relates to me, I think about all of the roads I've gone down in my lifetime. I've made some wrong turns but I thank God that He was right there with me the whole time. I've experienced heartache and heartbreak and again God has been with me through it all. He saw my tears and felt my pain. He keeps record of them so that He may remember and comfort me. Aren't you comforted by knowing that the Creator of the universe loves you enough to keep up with your wanderings and your tears?

God, how amazing is Your love for us! How awesome it is to know that You care so deeply for us that You store up our tears for remembrance purposes.

EXERCISE

Psalm 29:11

The LORD will give strength unto his people; the LORD will bless his people with peace

I imagine we all want to be stronger, physically, mentally, emotionally but most importantly spiritually. When we want to become stronger physically we do strength training; mentally, we play games or do things that will exercise our brains. Growing stronger spiritually requires training as well. Spending quality time in God's word will enable you to grow closer to Him. When you are in the Word, it becomes real to you and you begin to see new ways to apply it to your life. Having a daily prayer time will strengthen your relationship with God. The closer you are to God and the more you walk with Him the stronger you will become. He promised us in His word that He would give us strength to carry us on our journey. Start today off with some strength exercises!

Father, I'm so thankful that You give us Your promises, promises to strengthen us and to grow us stronger in You.

FINAL WORDS

Luke 23:24

Then said Jesus, Father, forgive them; for they know not what they do. And they parted his raiment, and cast lots.

The final thoughts of Jesus were of us. Breathing His last breath He asks our Heavenly Father to forgive them. Not only was Jesus asking God to forgive those that literally nailed him to the cross, but He was asking God to forgive us. Yes, He was looking 2000 years ahead and asking God to forgive you and me of the sins that we would commit. Wow! Can we even begin to understand what kind of grace was extended to us that day? To imagine that Christ, God's only son would have enough compassion to think of us as he was bleeding and dying.

Father, I can't comprehend the agony that You went through on the cross, I will never be able to understand how You could love me that much, but I am forever thankful that You did.

AMAZEMENT

Psalm 147:17

He casts forth his ice like morsels: who can stand before his cold?

Last night it hailed at my house. We had just gotten home and suddenly it sounded like a thousand horse hoofs on our metal roof. My family ran outside and watched as hail pounded the house and the cars. We've never seen it hail like that before. It probably only lasted five minutes but when it was over there was three inches of hail stones on our sidewalk. While I stood on the porch and watched it my mind went directly to scriptures. I thought about the times when hail was sent down in biblical times. Almost always something major was happening. God was showing up through the hail. Last night as my eyes were focused on the sky I kept saying things about the end times. I seriously expected the trumpet to sound and for Christ to gather His children to Him. It was a few moments of amazement at one of God's weather creations. There was still hail on my back deck when I got up this morning. Perhaps a reminder that God is always near and that one day we will witness many weather phenomenon as Christ appears!

God in heaven, I never cease to be amazed at all the things You created. You created rain, wind, snow and hail and You have total control over them all. Help us to not need reminders such as a hail storm to keep looking for Your coming.

A Worthy Walk

I Corinthians 1:10

I appeal to you, brothers, by the name of our Lord Jesus Christ, that all of you agree, and that there be no divisions among you, but that you be united in the same mind and the same judgment.

I will admit to you that I struggle with this every day. I allow my humanness to come into play way too often. Here Jesus was reminding the disciples to walk in a worthy way to which they were called. We are His disciples today. He wants us to stay united in Christian love and be an example of His love. When unbelievers see Christians fussing and back biting and gossiping about one another and others, it tears down our witness. With just a few words we can change someone's mind about accepting Jesus. Now, I know you don't think we hold that power but we do. When we treat someone poorly we are saying to that person that we don't respect them as one of God's children. While we are going about our everyday lives we are impressing others one way or the other. God calls us to point people toward Him. The old saying about being the only Bible some people read still holds true. Let people see Jesus in you!

Lord, I fail so many times while trying to live out this verse. Help us to stay united in Your love and to show people Your love even when it's difficult.

BEAUTY

1 Peter 3:4

> You should clothe yourselves instead with the beauty that comes from within, the unfading beauty of a gentle and quiet spirit, which is so precious to God.

Haven't we heard for years the saying "beauty is in the eye of the beholder"? Some of the most beautiful people I've ever known were the ones that had beautiful hearts. I'm not saying they weren't beautiful on the outside as well, but they just had sweet, meek hearts. They were humble and not boastful or full of themselves. Even as I've watched these individuals grow older they have grown more beautiful to me. You can tell their beauty comes from the One that lives in them, the one they fashion their life after. These friends are the ones that I find myself drawn to, the ones I choose to emulate. Why? Because they have something that will not fade with time. Today, take a look in your mirror but don't look at your face, take a deeper look into your heart! Beauty comes from the inside.

Lord, how thankful I am for beautiful friends in my life, those that have a heart for You and live each day showing me and others the way to You.

A Father's Love

Hosea 14:4

I will heal their backsliding, I will love them freely: for mine anger is turned away from him.

Do you remember when you were a kid and you disobeyed your parents? Maybe you didn't set out to disobey, it may have just happened. I was so blessed as a child. My parents were not hard on me. I was a pleaser and was really hard on myself when I made a mistake or did something wrong. I guess that is why my mom and dad went light on me. I can remember only a handful of times that I knew I disappointed my parents, mainly my dad. It just broke my heart if I failed my daddy. I would go to him in tears and cry my heart out before him asking his forgiveness. He would reach out and take me in his arms and hug away all of the hurt and things would be right again. How like God to give us earthly fathers as an example of His restoring love for us. God will restore us to right again when we go humbly to Him. He will not hold our wrongs over us or remind us of them again. He restores us with His love.

Father God, how grateful I am for Your restorative love. How many times, I've had to fall at Your feet and beg forgiveness. Thank You for always granting me another opportunity to serve You better.

Patience

Psalm 40:1

I waited patiently for the Lord; and he inclined unto me, and heard my cry.

When I think about this verse I think about patience. I don't have very much patience as a person. It's hard for me to wait on anyone to do my bidding or what I think they should be doing. This verse says, "I waited for the Lord." Do we? We are a generation of fixers. We think we can fix all of our own problems and most of the time we think that we can fix everyone else's as well. I tend to have that personality, let me give you my advice, let me tell you how I would do that. That attitude, however, is not from the Lord; the Lord wants us to wait on Him. Now I can tell you that is no easy task. Waiting for God to show us the way we need to go or answer a prayer that we've been putting out there for a while. However, this verse does tell us that He will hear our cry. It helps me so much to be able to go to the word and read that God, our Creator hears our cries! He wants us to cry out to Him for all that we need.

Lord, help us to seek shelter in Your provisions today! Help us to learn how to wait on Your answers.

Hero's

II Corinthians 10:4

For the weapons of our warfare *are* not carnal, but mighty through God to the pulling down of strong holds;

Today we see so many movies with heroes in them. Most kid's movies out have a central theme of someone being in distress and the hero saving the day. Did you know that as Christians we have a real live Hero? We have someone who has already stepped in and saved the day for us! Christ laid down His life so that we may have eternal life. Now He sits in heaven with God the Father and intercedes for us, on our behalf. We can give Him our battles and He will fight them for and with us. You can know for sure there is no battler bigger than God. Ultimately, our battle has already been fought and won and we are victors through Christ!

Lord, we can't begin to fathom what a great Hero You are in our lives. It is inconceivable that You would do something so amazing for us. Thank You for bringing us the ultimate victory no matter what battle we have to fight.

Restoration

John 11:4

When Jesus heard *that*, he said, This sickness is not unto death, but for the glory of God, that the Son of God might be glorified thereby.

The verse prior to this one is when Jesus finds out that Lazarus is sick. Over the course of the last year or so I've found out that several of my friends are suffering with sicknesses. Some of them have immune deficiencies that render their bodies helpless to fight off infection, some of them have multiple sclerosis that affects their central nervous system. Some of them are battling cancer of some form or other. It's so hard to see these sweet friends go through the effects of these diseases. How difficult it must be for them to remain hopeful in light of doctor's prognosis and continued pain. Martha and her family lost all hope when Lazarus died. However, hope was restored when Jesus raised Lazarus from the dead. In today's times we have not seen Jesus raise anyone from the dead, but we have seen God glorified when diseases have been healed and people's health have been restored. God can still restore health to sick, strength to weak and salvation to the lost.

Abba Daddy God, Who else holds the power of our very lives but You? We bow before You now Lord asking You to send restoration to those who are sick and weak.

CALLED

I Peter 2:9

But you are a chosen generation, a royal priesthood, an holy nation, a peculiar people; that you should show forth the praises of him who has called you out of darkness into his marvelous light;

He has called us! How amazing that is to me. To think that the Creator of the universe called us to him. Do you remember the day God called your name? I remember when he called mine! I was fifteen years old. He chose us to bless, protect and provide for. He set us apart as a Holy people known by His name, Christians! He called me and gave me eternal life. He knew that I was human and that I would make mistakes, but He loved me enough to call me anyway. That day he filled me with his light, the light that outshines all other light! He set me apart as His child.

Father, so many years ago You called me to walk with You and even though I've made many mistakes along the way You have walked faithfully with me on the journey and never let go of me.

Relinquished

Isaiah 41:10

Fear thou not; for I am with thee: be not dismayed; for I am thy God: I will strengthen thee; yea, I will help thee; yea, I will uphold thee with the right hand of my righteousness.

This is my favorite verse in the Bible and I'm so thankful for it. I have shared it with many friends during hard times. I can visualize how God will lift us up and give us physical, emotional and spiritual strength and it becomes very personal to me. Don't you love that the very first words are "fear not"? You see God knows that the first thing we feel when our life is out of control is fear. When we can relinquish our fear then we have room to feel the strength of God as He tends to our needs. I can almost hear God as he speaks this verse to my broken heart. Can't you see God leaning down and scooping you up and holding you in His hand? What better place to be when our lives are turned upside down?

Father, this verse speaks to my heart like no other. All of the emotions we feel when our lives fall apart are healed by You. How blessed we are to have this promise.

SECURED

Romans 6:23

For the wages of sin [is] death; but the gift of God [is] eternal life through Jesus Christ our Lord.

Today, I was talking to a friend of mine whose daughter had received some disturbing news. We started talking about others that are going through trials. The thought came to me that no matter what else happens in our lives, today, tomorrow or beyond if we have Jesus in our hearts then nothing else matters. Yes, we will still have trails and things will upset us. God knows as humans we are going to hurt, be afraid and be downhearted. The good news is that he will walk with us through all of that. When it's all said and done and our walk here is over, we will get to see Him face to face. We will hear Him call our name to come to Him for eternity. In light of this promise we can have hope.

Lord, today as I have prayed for several hurting people I am thankful that You hear our prayers, but mostly I'm thankful that those that I am praying for are Your children and that nothing on this earth can separate them from You.

WEARY

Jeremiah 31:25

For I have satiated the weary soul, and I have replenished every sorrowful soul.

Are you struggling? Do you ever feel like you just can't take another step? Another breath? You just can't go on trudging through this life you are living. Your Creator wants to give you supernatural strength to carry on. He promised you that He would fill you up again. Why do we so often wait to go to Him until He is our last resort? Wouldn't it be so much easier to go to Him to begin with? He waits on you to come to Him. He loves you so much, and He wants to be first in your life all of the time. He longs to share every part of your life. Run to Him when you are weary and downtrodden. He will welcome you with open arms!

Lord, what an amazing promise to Your children. You will give us strength when we need it to continue forward. Thank You for holding us up when we can't go alone.

FORMED

Isaiah 64:8

But now, O LORD, thou *art* our father; we *are* the clay, and thou our potter; and we all *are* the work of thy hand.

Have you ever dabbled in pottery or watched a potter at work? It's an amazing trade and takes a lot of time and patience. There are many steps in perfecting the beautiful vessels that are formed. We are all formed by God and He formed each of us in a unique way. He took time to mold us into the exact vessel that He wants us to be. The potter starts with a piece of unmolded clay and works on that clay until the vision for that clay has been achieved. In the final steps a piece of pottery has a glaze applied to prepare it to hold liquids and not leak. In the last step of the process the clay must be heated to set it, making it strong for its purpose, enabling it to be used for whatever purpose the potter chose for that piece. The pieces formed are used for many purposes. Our Father is the ultimate Potter. We are God's vessels and He created each of us for a purpose. If you haven't found your purpose yet, call out to God and ask Him to use your vessel for His glory and His purpose.

Father God, how amazing to think that You could form us from the very beginning and that You spent time making us just how You wanted us to be. You thought enough of us to give each of us a work to do for You. Please help us to always be a willing vessel for You.

Parched

Exodus 15:27

And they came to Elim, where *were* twelve wells of water, and threescore and ten palm trees: and they encamped there by the waters.

Are you in a desert? So many of us find ourselves in the dry parched climate of the desert. We can't seem to find a way to the next spring of water. We are too parched to get up and use what little energy we have left to go forward. When we, like the Israelites, are in need of strength to stay on the journey we will find that God is our oasis. God physically led them to an oasis where they camped and were refreshed so they could continue on. God will lead you to an oasis too. He will give you renewed strength to stay on the path and to make it through to the end.

Lord, I'm so thankful that just like You led the Israelites to an oasis, You are here to refresh us when we can't keep going. Thank You for walking with us and giving us strength for each day along our journey.

RICHES

Ephesians 2:7

That in the ages to come he might shew the exceeding riches of his grace in *his* kindness toward us through Christ Jesus.

Satan has this lie that he loves to spread around. He likes to make us think that God doesn't love us or the things that we've done are unforgivable. He tells the lie that we've gone too far this time and that God won't forgive us. Aren't we all beyond grateful that God proved the devil to be a liar! God sent His precious son Jesus to be payment for our sins. The ones that we have already committed and the ones that we will commit in the future. That is God's unfathomable grace extended to us when we are His! God not only forgives those sins but He forgets them as well. We must not fall victim to the devils lies anymore!

God, I am so thankful that no matter how many times the devil rears his ugly head we have Your promise that he has been eternally defeated! There are no words to express my thankfulness.

The Word

Psalm 119:11

Thy word have I hid in mine heart, that I might not sin against thee.

Is God's word in your house? In my home I have several plaques, pictures and crosses that depict verses from the Bible. So yes, in my case, the Word really is in my house. I like having those reminders of my faith in my home. I don't do it to be showy or to prove any points. It's just what is in my heart so I enjoy allowing it to overflow into my home. However, there is an even more important place that we need to have the Word and that is in our hearts. I'm not speaking of salvation here, I'm speaking of the scriptures that God gave us as our guide. I have found the more I delve into God's word and hide it away in my heart the more equipped I am to use it. Often times, I need a scripture to come to my mind when sin comes knocking on my door! Sometimes, I need a scripture to encourage someone along the way. How could you use the scriptures that you have hidden in your heart today?

Lord, thank You for Your scriptures to guide our pathways. Remind us of them when sin comes into our realm and help us to use them to help others.

SHINE

Matthew 5:16

Let your light so shine before men, that they may see your good works, and glorify your Father which is in heaven.

I love the old song "The Lighthouse". When I think about that song I think how God is my light! He is my guide and will never guide me the wrong way. We can be a lighthouse in a dark world today. We can guide others to the light that never fades. I can imagine the days when ships were at sea and the storms raged and the captains looked anxiously for the light on the hillside to guide them to safety. There are many people in this world today looking for a guide. What an amazing opportunity we have to be God's light and their lighthouse, directing them to safety and peace and hope.

Father, don't let me miss an opportunity to be a light for You and to guide others toward the safety of Your arms.

Stop, Look and Listen

Romans 15:13

Now the God of hope fill you with all joy and peace in believing, that ye may abound in hope, through the power of the Holy Ghost.

Stop, look and listen! As Christians, we have the most wonderful gift to share! We have hope in Christ! This hope offers joy and peace. It brings comfort and encouragement. We live in a frantic world and it seems like we live our days running from one task to another. How often do we take time to stop and see what is really going on around us? Do we take time to look around us to see the needs of others? Do we really listen to what is being said? In a world where so many of our friends and co-workers are hurting we have the opportunity to share God's love and His hope.

Thank You Father for Your gift of hope. Help us Lord to share it with others along the way.

The Lamb

John 1:29

The next day John seeth Jesus coming unto him, and saith, Behold the Lamb of God, which taketh away the sin of the world.

The words "Mary had a little lamb, its fleece was white as snow" has long been known as a nursery rhyme. Long before that nursery rhyme was written a young girl named Mary gave birth to a son. Truly, we know that the little boy Mary gave birth to that day was the Lamb of God. Spotless and without blemish, He was born to take away our sins. How unworthy we are to be saved by this Lamb, but how magnificent that we can obtain eternal life through Him! Holy Holy is the Lamb of God!

Father God, worthy is the Lamb! Praise and honor to Him!

JUDGING

John 8:7

So when they continued asking him, he lifted up himself, and said unto them, He that is without sin among you, let him first cast a stone at her.

Are you a stone thrower? *NO!* That is probably your answer. I bet if you stop to think about it though you've probably hurled a few. Wow! We tend to believe everything we hear about people. The juicier the gossip the better. However, it is not our place to judge even when we hear something that may be true. I learned a valuable lesson a long time ago, when I went through something very personal. There were many of my friends that prayed for me without failing during the situation, but there were stone throwers as well and yes some of them were Christians! Some relationships were torn apart and friendships lost that have never been repaired or will never be quite the same. Since then I have had this quirky saying "I don't throw stones because I've lived in a glass house". During all of this I found solace in a God that never stopped loving me and forgave me every time I needed him too.

Father, thank You for Your forgiveness and for the reminder that none of us are without sin.

THE GREAT COMMISSION

Acts 1:8

But you shall receive power, after the Holy Spirit has come upon you: and you shall be witnesses unto me both in Jerusalem, and in all Judea, and in Samaria, and unto the uttermost part of the earth.

God gave us a directive to go and witness and he equipped us with the power to do it. I don't know why it is then that we are so afraid of actually carrying out the act of witnessing. There are many ways to witness. However, when we think about witnessing, we tend to think about verbally sharing the gospel. This is of course the great commission for Christians, to share God's love. We are witnesses' everyday even if we don't think about it. Most of us are around people all day at work or school. How we respond to situations is a big expression of our faith. When someone lashes out at us or hurts our feelings. When things don't go as planned. When our car won't crank and we are late for work. What about when someone is telling an off-colored joke? Do you walk away or do you join in and laugh? Is someone in need? Do we ignore that need or do we try to meet it? You may not feel you can walk up to a stranger and tell them about God but you are a witness for God in every act that you do.

God, I pray that You will help me to be a better witness for You, help me to pay attention to the needs of others, and to be bolder about my faith.

WWJD

I Peter 2:24

Who his own self bare our sins in his own body on the tree, that we, being dead to sins, should live unto righteousness: by whose stripes ye were healed.

A few years ago the big saying going around in the Christian circle was "WWJD or What Would Jesus Do?" I used that phase a good many times myself when a decision would come my way. However, looking back maybe the better question would have been. What DID Jesus do? He was born in a lowly stable, He was tempted by the devil but lived a sinless life. He bore OUR sins when He died on the cross. He became our only method of reaching Heaven. He interceded for us then and He became our intercessor between us and God. Through Jesus our prayers go straight to the Father! Maybe the next time that you hear "WWJD" you might turn it around to WDJD! Don't you stand amazed that He did all of this for us! I do!

Father in Heaven, thank You for giving up Your Son for me. What a sacrifice You made even though I was not worthy nor will ever be.

Hunger

I Peter 2:2

As newborn babes, desire the sincere milk of the word, that ye may grow thereby:

Are you hungry? We get physically hungry all of the time. What about being spiritually hungry? I know that the reason we are supposed to eat is to sustain our bodies, but let's be honest, most of us love to eat. Our body is geared to let us know when we need food to nourish it. We have to have food to give our body the energy it needs to function. Most of us don't like to skip meals, but we don't have a problem with skipping out on feeding from God's word. We need to feed the spiritual part of our bodies. We need to get into God's word on a daily basis. We will be in such better shape to go out and work for God when our spiritual body has been fed. Let's get in a habit of feeding our bodies, hearts, minds and souls daily.

Lord, I pray that as our physical bodies grow hungry that we will remember that we need re-filling spiritually as well.

Direction

Psalm 48:14

For this God *is* our God for ever and ever: he will be our guide *even* unto death.

In my morning prayers I always ask God to be my Pilot. I mean this literally while I am on the road in my car and in every aspect of my day. When we give God full reign over our days first thing then we don't have to worry about anything that happens. We know that no matter the circumstances, He will be in control and that He knows what's best for us. Isn't it freeing to give him all of your worries and insecurities and be done with it? In the morning when you get up ask him to be your Pilot as well. I promise you the ride will be so much easier and rewarding!

Father, thank You for being my Pilot every day. Thank You for reminding me that when I allow You to, You will take charge of my life and lead me each mile.

Confidence

I John 5:14

And this is the confidence that we have in him, that, if we ask any thing according to his will, he heareth us:

I think about God up there in Heaven and how He already knows what we are going to ask for, but He wants us to ask anyway. He wants us to come to Him like a child comes to their daddy and lay our hearts at His feet. So as this verse says we need to pray earnestly expecting great things from God. When I was growing up my cousins would come down from another part of the state almost every weekend. In the summer as the weekend drew to a close it was an inevitable question that we were going to pose to see if they could stay a week or two with my grandparents. The cousins always put me up to asking because they knew the request would have a better outcome for me than them. You see most of the time their dad had already instructed them on the way down "not to ask" about staying. So I ask the question and many times he gave in and allowed them to stay for a visit. I think about him when I read this verse. He knew that I would keep asking every time they visited all summer long. Keep on asking God for your heart's desires.

God, thank You that You never grow tired us our request, no matter how often we come to You with them.

LISTENING

Psalm 46:10

Be still, and know that I am God: I will be exalted among the heathen, I will be exalted in the earth.

Are you listening? We are always so full of words, dying to tell someone the latest news. Eager to speak up and share something that is going on in our lives. I find I'm like that with God too. I want to get down on my knees and get down to business about my business! I rattle on and on not taking into consideration what God may want to tell me. After all prayer is a conversation with God and we can't have a conversation when one of us is speaking the entire time. The next time that you have prayer, just listen for a spell and see what God has to say to you.

Father, I am so thankful You listen to my prayers, but I'm even more thankful that You want to speak to me.

Serenade

Genesis 1:21

And God created great whales, and every living creature that moveth, which the waters brought forth abundantly, after their kind, and every winged fowl after his kind: and God saw that it was good.

Last night my family was sitting at the dinner table eating when I heard them. The frogs! I shushed my family from their talking and said "listen!" We have a pool and at the beginning of every summer the frogs come to stay and serenade us. I love to hear their beautiful song. The frogs were singing their melodic song and they sang right through dinner on into the night. As I fell asleep I could still hear them. I'm always amazed at God's creations and the varied ways that we are able to enjoy it. Something as simple as the frogs singing their summer song gives me great joy.

Thank You God for the frogs, thank You for the beautiful season that they announce and their beautiful music as I fall asleep.

CALM

I Corinthians 14:33

For God is not the author of confusion, but of peace, as in all churches of the saints.

Why is it that we let the world come in and try to tangle us up and destroy us? The Lord doesn't want us to be tied up in knots over situations. He wants us to trust him in everything. His way is plain and straight. His way doesn't lead to hatred, back biting and hurt feelings. Satan is the one that thrives on these things. He pits us against one another, he puts hateful thoughts and words into our minds and mouths. He stirs the pot every chance he gets. He loves for us to be confused and not have our focus on Jesus and His ways. The next time you are feeling confused because the world has been biting at your heels, just remember that Satan has been eternally defeated and God is the victor always and forever!

Thank You God that when the world seems in mass chaos and our feelings are in turmoil You give us a calm peace for our hearts and souls.

COURAGE

Deuteronomy 31:6

Be strong and of good courage, do not fear nor be afraid of them; for the LORD your God, He *is* the One who goes with you. He will not leave You nor forsake You.

I love this verse so much. I think this is one of those verses I need taped to my bathroom mirror. I need to read it at the beginning of each new day. I believe gaining the strength and the courage to face each new day must come from the Lord! If you believe that anything on earth is going to give you what you need to make it in today's world then I believe you are going to be disappointed. God already has your day planned out. In fact, He already has your life planned out. He created you in His likeness so He cares about what happens to you. He will go before you and with you while you go through your day. All you have to do is ask Him to guide you and to direct your steps in His ways. No matter what today holds for you, you can be sure that God will be there and that He will not leave you. We have His promise!

God, thank You for providing for us each new day. Thank You that we don't have to go through our days alone.

HONOR

Romans 12:10

Be kindly affectioned one to another with brotherly love;
in honour preferring one another;

I try not to be selfish, but sometimes I'm pretty sure I am. I am a creature of habit, and like things a certain way. However many of my friends would probably tell you that I'm pretty flexible. I have *the more the merrier* attitude when it comes to getting together with friends. I quickly jump in and try to help. My trouble comes when I'm extending grace toward people by assisting them in areas of their lives or helping to build them up again! My heart's desire is to be there for anyone who needs me, but then I find myself growing weary of being the do-gooder. I know that is from the physical aspect and not a spiritual one. It's in these times that I have to take a step back and look to the scriptures to guide my steps and give me grace and love so that I can continue to be Jesus' hands and feet on this earth.

Lord, I want to always be the vessel that You use to reach others, but I fail so many times. I ask that You give me the physical and spiritual strength to stay the course.

SUPPLIER

Philippians 4:19

But my God shall supply all your need according to his riches in glory by Christ Jesus.

Do we know the difference in a need and a want? I venture to say that many of us don't. Somewhere along the line we have come to believe that we are entitled to everything we want. We also have a hard time with delayed gratification. In other words, we want what we want and we want it now! Make yourself a check list of real needs and be literal. Mine would look like this: air to breathe, food to eat, clothes to wear, a roof over my head, transportation, a job so I can pay for these things. Those are my physical needs, but I have many more. I have a need to be loved, a need to be healthy, and a need for my family to be united and well and so on. I believe that God knows each thing we need way before we do. I have full faith that He will provide for us just like His word tells us. He has proved it to me over and over again. Give God your list of needs and let Him provide for you.

Lord, I'm so grateful that You supply all of my needs and You allow me have many of my wants. You always amaze me with Your love.

Claim It

Psalm 103:12

As far as the east is from the west, so far has he removed our transgressions from us.

This is one of those verses I pray back to God. When I pray in the mornings before my day starts I remember this verse and claim it for that day. Knowing that no matter what I have done, God has removed it from me. God not only removes our sins from us but He forgets about them! Completely forgets, not to bring them up to us again. He doesn't throw them in our faces the next time we sin. He keeps no record of them at all. Satan is the one that brings our past back to us; he's the one with the tape recorder he re-winds over and over again. He wants us to believe we are useless to God and that our sins will keep us from God. That is not true! God gave us Jesus and Jesus defeated Satan! No words from Satan are true. He is the deceiver and he wants to destroy you, especially when you start really living for God. Keep claiming God's word, keep remembering these important verses that God gave us. God is the victor!

Father God, I fail so many times, but God You are faithful to forgive me each time and restore me back to You. Thank You God!

WHOLE

Luke 8:48

And he said unto her, Daughter, be of good comfort: thy faith hath made thee whole; go in peace

Jesus is in the healing business. How do I know? Jesus was on his way to heal a child, the crowds were great, people pressing up against him, wanting to touch him. A woman had been to doctors seeking healing but no healing could be found. For twelve years she had looked for answers. Her faith was strong and she knew that if she could just touch Jesus that she would be healed. She planned only to touch Him, not feeling worthy to address Him. She reached out and touched the hem of His robe. Healing powers left Him and He asked who had touched Him. The woman was pointed out and Jesus said to her, "Woman your faith has made you whole". That unnamed woman had a lot of faith! Do we exhibit that kind of faith when we go before God? We know that we can place our needs at His feet and leave them there and that He will take care of them. We have to have the faith to do it.

God, help our faith to be as strong as this woman. Help us to reach for the hem of Your garment in our time of need.

Safe

Psalm 56:3

What time I am afraid, I will trust in thee.

A few years ago we had a sudden snowstorm hit our little town. It started with just a few flurries and before long the roads became white and were quickly becoming impassable. I work at a school close to my home and at that time my daughter worked at another school about 30 minutes away. It started snowing here before it did there and I called to let her know that our school was dismissing. Since it was not snowing where she was, she was surprised. Within the hour however, it begin snowing there. I made it home from work, though the roads were bad. Keep in mind that she was further away so it took her much longer to make it home. Since we don't have snow very often she had never driven in these conditions. The first thing I did when I got home was go get my Bible and get down on my knees and pray for her protection. I walked the floors for the long hour or so that it took her to arrive, holding my Bible and praying constantly. God knew that I was afraid for my daughter's safety and I knew I had to put my trust in Him to take care of her.

Lord, thank You that You know our fears and that You care about what we care about. Thank You for Your divine protection that day and everyday!

Divine Intervention

Psalm 91:11

For he shall give his angels charge over thee, to keep thee in all thy ways.

Several years ago my mom called me and said she wasn't feeling well. I live close by her home so I rushed over carrying my daughter, Katlin with me. My mom was having trouble breathing when we got there and was in bad distress. I knew something had to be done quickly. I grabbed the phone and dialed 911. While I was on the phone with them giving them details my mom was getting worse. I instructed Katlin who was probably about ten or eleven at the time to go out to the edge of my mom's yard and try to wave someone down from the road. You see, we live in a rural area on a country road so there wasn't much traffic coming by. Almost immediately a truck came by as my sweet girl stood out there screaming and flailing her arms. The truck whipped into the drive and the driver asked Katlin what the problem is. They came into the house together and he immediately took over the care of my mom, telling me he was a paramedic! A little later the ambulance arrived and carried my mom to the hospital where she made a full recovery. I often reflect back on that time and how although I didn't even pray right then, God knew my heart! He knew that I needed help and He sent it and not just anyone but a paramedic. He sent us an Angel that day to keep my mom alive! I will always be in awe of the love that He showed us that day.

Abba Daddy God, Thank You for providing just what we need just when we need it. Thank You for sending me one of Your Angels that day!

Multi Task

Psalm 17:6

I have called upon thee, for thou wilt hear me, O God: incline thine ear unto me, *and hear* my speech.

Think about all of the things that you have to accomplish in a day. Cook, clean, work, shuffle kids back and forth, and answer a million questions from your kids along the way. Sometime it just gets more than we feel like we can handle. We have to stop the roller coaster and get off for a few minutes to re-group. God never has to re-group. I am always amazed that no matter that He might be listening to thousands of people at one time, He still hears my prayer! Much like we are with our children when we are cooking dinner, washing clothes or helping with homework. We are completing multiple tasks at a time. God does that with ease and never grows tired or complains because too many things are being thrown his way at once. That, folks, is God's amazing love!

God thank You that You are never too busy for me, and that You never grow tired of my request.

GIVE IT UP

John 14:27

Peace I leave with you, My peace I give to you; not as the world gives do I give to you. Let not your heart be troubled, neither let it be afraid.

My daughter and I have always been very close. As she grew up it was especially hard for this mother to let her become an adult. When it came time for her to decide where she was going to college, she had two schools in mind. One was a school in a nearby city and one was about two hours away. The thought of my sweet baby girl moving two hours away to live and go to school struck fear in my heart! It wasn't that I didn't think she could do it. It was because I, being selfish didn't want her to go. We had many arguments about the decision and finally one day it came to me. *I have got to give this to God completely!* I started praying for peace. I prayed that whatever decision she made that God would give me complete peace about it. I tried to back away and let her decide without giving her problems. It wasn't long after I prayed my prayer that I heard her tell someone she was going to stay home and attend the nearby college. My heart leapt with joy! I was thankful that this time her decision was the one I wanted her to make, but I was more thankful that God had given me peace while waiting on her to decide.

God, You always know what is best for Your children, we don't have to be afraid when we seek You for our answers.

Speak Up

Mark 16:15

And he said unto them, Go ye into all the world, and preach the gospel to every creature.

Have you ever missed an opportunity to witness? I mean the one when you walked away you knew that you should have spoken up. Years ago, I missed an opportunity to share my faith with a gentlemen. I can still see it in my mind. I work at a school and this man had come to pick up his daughter from school. I don't remember his specific circumstances but he was having a bad day. He and his daughter left the building and I didn't think anything else about it. I left for home just a few minutes later and was surprised to see him and his daughter on the playground. I felt the tug of the Holy Spirit so strong to stop and approach them, to talk to him about what was going on and tell him about Christ. I ignored it and kept on driving. To this day I wonder about him and that little girl. She was still in my school but I don't remember him ever coming to pick her up again. I missed the opportunity that God placed right before me. I will regret my decision forever and will always wonder what change might have been brought about had I listened to God. I had to repent for not being obedient and God forgave me, but I will always carry that lesson with me. God places us where we are for a purpose. As I continue to grow in God's love, I try to be more observant and obedient when God gives me opportunities to share his love.

God, You know I've already repented from the sin of disobedience. I thank You God that You have given me more opportunities to be bold for You.

REACH OUT

Luke 14:23

And the lord said unto the servant, Go out into the highways and hedges, and compel *them* to come in, that my house may be filled.

Yesterday I was in a small store close to my home, when I encountered a gentleman that seemed to need some help. He was on the same isle as I was and couldn't find what he needed. He looked at me and said, "I don't know much about this store, I'm new in town." Normally, in this situation I would have asked what he was looking for, helped him to locate it and went on my way. However, I struck up a conversation with him, asking where he lived and worked. He and his wife had just moved here and he had been working in their yard. I told him that if he and his wife were looking for a church we would love for them to visit our church and told him the service times. About that time my husband came around the isle and they introduced themselves to one another and continued to talk. Interestingly enough, the man worked at a place where my husband had worked years ago. After a few more minutes we went on our way with a wave of goodbye. I don't know if the gentleman and his wife will visit our church or not, but I stepped out of my comfort zone for Christ yesterday. It may not seem like a big thing to you but I believe that God put me and that man in the same store on the same isle at the same time for a purpose. I just had to be obedient in God's plan.

God, thank You for using me to share Your love and invite people to Your house to grow closer to You.

Sight Restored

Luke 18:43

And immediately he received his sight, and followed Him, glorifying God. And all the people, when they saw *it,* gave praise to God.

A few years ago, my husband started having trouble with his right eye. His vision seemed blocked by a curtain. We went to our eye doctor where he was told that he had dry eye syndrome and was given drops. His vision didn't improve after using the drops for several days, so we went back to the doctor. After an exam the doctor immediately diagnosed him with a detached retina. We were sent that afternoon to see a surgeon and he was scheduled for surgery that week. Before the surgery she gave us the scenarios that we were facing. Complete blindness in that eye was a real possibility. Thankfully, the surgery was a success, but the journey was far from over. My husband spent over a week lying face down, only able to get up to use the restroom. He had a bubble placed in his eye and it had to stay at a certain level at all times, this meant he could only sit and lie in certain positions. He spent a month having 5 different drops placed in his eye 5 or 6 times a day. He had to go to the doctor every week for weeks, then once a month for an entire year. When the pressure in his eye was too high at doctor's visits, he had to have shots in his eye to lower it. He missed about 2 months of work. After diligently following the directions of his surgeon and praying that God would restore his sight he made a full recovery. We were so thankful that God led us to the right surgeon and watched over her and my husband during the surgery. We know that God restored his sight just as he restored the sight of blind men in the Bible.

God, I thank You that You are still in the miracle business and that You gave my husband the miracle of restored sight!

Rest

Matthew 11:28

Come unto me, all you that labor and are heavy laden,
and I will give you rest.

When I was growing up we didn't have air conditioning in our home. On those early summer days we would be out working in the yard and cleaning up around the house. There would be this wonderful breeze blowing and I would sneak away to my room where the windows were wide open and lay down across my bed and fall asleep after working outside. It was the best rest ever. The bed was soft, the breeze was cool and I, an innocent child, could lay all my cares aside and rest. Today we are a generations of "doers". We hardly ever take time to rest; we fall into the bed at night exhausted and spent from the day. God wants us to lay down our burdens and our chores for a while and just rest. His desire is for us to lay down as a child and surrender into His rest.

Thank You father that You give us time in the day to stop our toiling and to rest in You. Help us to remember that resting is part of Your plan and even You rested after creating the earth.

RENEWAL

Psalm 119:62

At midnight I will rise to give thanks unto thee because of thy righteous judgments.

Have you ever been wide awake at night and started praying? When I am unable to sleep I start going down my prayer list in my mind, praying for each need. I spend some time praising God for his wonderful blessings. I love that people in biblical times prayed in the night as well. You will find some very significant things that happened in the Bible at midnight. It is believed to be a special time of night according to commentaries. Not only did people bow before God at midnight to worship him but major things happened at that hour. If you will search the scriptures you will find that God used the midnight hour to start something new in people's lives. (Exodus 11-4 and Ruth 3-8). It was a time of renewing and starting over. It was a time when hope was restored, prayers answered and lives changed. God gave many directives at midnight. Even though it was the darkest hour, many blessings were given beginning the new day. The next time you find yourself unable to sleep and are tossing and turning at midnight, start thinking about what new joy you will have in the morning!

Lord, we thank You that You took the darkest hour of the night and turned it into a time to look past to see what change and joy You will bring in the new day. Thank You for all of our days and nights.

SHELTER

Psalm 18:2

The LORD is my rock and my fortress and my deliverer;
My God, my strength, in whom I will trust; My shield and
the horn of my salvation, my stronghold.

From the time I started writing this devotion book, I knew the title would be "My Shelter". Many times in my Christian life I have sought shelter in my Father's arms. He is my rock, stable and unmoving, He is my deliverer, the One that set me free from sin and hell. My Shield that protects me from the arrows of this world. He is my stronghold, the One that I can cling to through all of life's trials and even into death. Each time I think of the word shelter, I see God's hands. Sometimes, they are spread out over me to hide from the storms that are crashing around me. At other times, they are cupped, holding me up when I'm too weary or broken to continue on the journey. No matter what is happening in my life, God is in control and He will shelter me through it all.

Father God, thank You for providing every kind of shelter for me and protecting me throughout the days of my life.

He Holds Us

Zephaniah 3:17

The LORD thy God in the midst of thee *is* mighty; he will save, he will rejoice over thee with joy; he will rest in his love, he will joy over thee with singing.

Can you get a clear picture of God's love for us? From the beginning of His life until His last breath He was destined to die because of His love for us. It wasn't nails that held Him to that cross, it was His love for us. He didn't just save us from hell, He called us to Him, to be His own. He doesn't want us to suffer and He rejoices with us when we are happy. In Him we can find a rest that can't be found anywhere else. Just as a parent might hold their tired child close to their breast and sing them a lullaby, Jesus does that for us. He wants to hold us close to Him, to satisfy our needs and give us our hearts desires. What a love that is! An unfathomable love that goes beyond words.

Lord, just to think how You care about us, to think how You want to be personal with us and be in the midst of everything that we think and do is overwhelming to me. How great You are my father!

GOSSIP

Isaiah 40:28

Hast thou not known? hast thou not heard, *that* the everlasting God, the LORD, the Creator of the ends of the earth, fainteth not, neither is weary? *there is* no searching of his understanding.

Wow! My 13 year old granddaughter and a friend of hers are writing a devotion for a program at their school. This morning I asked her what it was on and she said on having faith in God. This is one of the verses they are using. How amazingly simple! It's like we are sharing a little bit of juicy gossip. Have you not heard? Where have you been? Don't you know that God is the Creator of the universe? He has always been here from the beginning and He will be here forever. He is an all knowing, all seeing awesome God! We can have faith in Him because He is in total control of everything in our lives. He never grows too tired to take care of us. How is it that there are people in this world that do not know this? How can we keep from shouting it from our roof tops? We serve a wonderful, loving, forgiving, everlasting God! Sharing this kind of news should be easy for us. We should be thrilled to be able to give everyone we see this news. What a difference it could make in the lives of those around us. Hast thou not known? Hast thou not heard?

Lord, why is it so hard for us to share such amazing news with the people around us? We should be shouting to the top of our lungs about Your awesomeness! Help us to give You the glory and praise for who You are in our lives and to share You with everyone we see.

MASTER

Mark 4:39

And he arose, and rebuked the wind, and said unto the sea, Peace, be still. And the wind ceased, and there was a great calm.

This morning as I prepare to attend and assist with the wedding of a very close friend, I am keeping my ear tuned to the weather station. They are predicting strong to severe storms during the timeline of her outdoor wedding. As I shoot up another prayer to God asking him to please give us good weather for those few hours and to keep us safe this day, I hear the words "He is the master of the wind" echo in my mind. I'm so thankful that no matter what the weathermen may say or what the radar may show that ultimately my God has total control over the weather. Many of her friends have prayed for the weather to be stable today. Now we must put our faith to work and believe God will provide.

God, I am more than thankful that when we place our days in Your hands You will carry us through them according to Your plan. I pray for this day to hold good weather for my friend.

HURTING

Psalm 6:2

Have mercy upon me, O Lord; for I am weak: O Lord heal me; for my bones are vexed.

These last few days have been a challenge for so many of my coworkers. We are a close knit group and share many of our problems and joys together. Recently, it just seems the troubles have outweighed the joys. Sweet Christian friends have been hurting, because they are watching their loved one hurt. Some of them are holding vigil with sick and dying parents. Some are transporting their sick children back and forth to doctors and getting no answers and seeing no improvement. Its times like these our defenses are down and we need the reassurance of God's love and care. Yesterday, a friend was saying how much she needed God to intervene for her and others. We are weak before an Almighty God, the One who loves us and will not fail us. In our weakness He shines. It's these moments that we must claim this verse and leave all of our hurts and cares to our Father.

Lord, You know how quickly this world can swallow us up. I pray God for You to extend your hand of mercy and heal our sick ones. Give us physical and emotional strength for the days ahead.

Know Peace

Isaiah 26:12

Lord, thou wilt ordain peace for us: for thou also hast wrought all our works in us.

Tonight after a long day of pulling double duty at work, I came home and just wanted a few minutes to myself to rest. However, my Poodle, Yorkie and cat had other ideas, as they were all clamoring for my attention. A bit exasperated I said out loud "No peace!" Then it hit me. I can't have peace from the animals until I show them some attention. Isn't that true with God as well? We can't have peace from him if we don't show Him some attention! We must truly know God to have peace from Him. My furry friends know me and they seek me to meet their needs and give them peace from their worries and anxieties. How like God to give us charge over His creatures to teach a lesson about His love for us.

Father, thank You that You give me Your peace just when I need it, and thank You for using Your creation to remind me that I can share that peace.

CRYING

Revelation 21:4

And God shall wipe away all tears from their eyes; and there shall be no more death, neither sorrow, nor crying, neither shall there be any more pain: for the former things are passed away.

Are you tired of crying? There was a time in my life that I felt like I cried more than anything else. I was broken from loss and when I was alone I would cry. I don't cry often and I usually don't cry in front of people, even my closest friends. This was right after my mom went to Heaven and I couldn't get past losing my best friend. I would write her letters almost every day. It was a great way for me to mourn and heal. I looked to God in a way I had never done before for peace and healing. He never let me cry alone and He whispered His sweet promises to me in my darkest times. Whatever is going on in your life, know that God will walk with you through it. He will wipe your tears away while on this earth and one day we will live with Him in a place where there are no tears, no pain, no sorrow and no death. We can claim these promises on our journey to that home.

Lord, I'm so thankful that even when I could not see ahead, that You dried my tears and kept holding me. I thank You that one day we will live with You eternally where there will be no more tears.

Serve

Jonah 1:17

Now the LORD had prepared a great fish to swallow up Jonah. And Jonah was in the belly of the fish three days and three nights.

What's swallowing you up and keeping you from doing God's will? There are so many excuses we use to keep from really taking on what He has laid out for us to do. I guess nothing quite as drastic as being swallowed by a large fish will happen if we let our opportunities to serve go by, but something will happen. It may not even be noticeable but when we don't seize the opportunities that God places before us, we lose out. He places people in our lives for specific reasons and certain times. He was sending Jonah to Nineveh, but Jonah was afraid. We are probably afraid sometimes, too. After a short vacation in the belly of that fish, Jonah decided to try it God's way. We can learn from Jonah's mistake and always be willing and ready for God's directive for our lives.

Lord, I thank You for the opportunity to serve You, I am amazed that You chose me with all of my humanness to reach out to others for You.

UNSINKABLE

Matthew 8:26

And he said to them, "Why are you afraid, O you of little faith?" Then he rose and rebuked the winds and the sea, and there was a great calm.

I have a quote on my computer at work that says "To have God on our side doesn't mean sailing on a boat with no storms, it means having a boat that no storm can sink". I have shared this quote with a lot of my friends over time. It's just there to remind me that no matter how many storms come or how bad they are I have faith in the one that calms them all. I am talking about real storms, such as tornados and hurricanes, and I'm referring to the storms in our lives. The ones that rock our very being and leave us torn up inside. Our God has total power and control over everything that happens. He knows before each storm hits that it's coming. It's up to us to choose to allow Him to calm the seas during these storms. Even those closest to Jesus doubted His ability to calm the seas but He did it for them. He will do it for you too! Trust in Him to handle the storm you are in today.

Lord, I thank You that nothing happens in our lives that You aren't in control of. I thank You for calming the storms in my life.

WILLING

Luke 22:34

And he said, I tell thee, Peter, the cock shall not crow this day, before that thou shalt thrice deny that thou knowest me.

We all deny Christ, maybe not as blatantly as Peter did, but we still do it. I constantly tell my husband that God has him in the place he works for a specific reason. There are people that he works with every day that need to know God. In his everyday business he has the opportunity to show others Christ in his life. We all do. Our Christian witness doesn't end at the church door or when the prayer meeting is over. It should begin then! We have so much power that God has given us to share His love and His word. He equips those of us that are willing to share. Peter was a loved disciple and wanted to be with Jesus day and night, yet Satan took him over for a time and he denied Christ. Satan is alive and well in our world today and he is eager to take us over. After Peter denied Christ he was ashamed and deeply disturbed at what he had done, but praise be to God, He forgave Peter of his sin and sent him on a mission. God will do the same for us. Through Jesus, He will save our souls from hell, He will equip us to work for him and He will forgive us when we fail. How great is our God!

Lord, thank You for the reminder that even those closest to failed You. As humans our flesh is weak and we mess us so many times. I so thankful for Your beautiful mercy and grace to redeem me.

GRATITUDE

Matthew 21:22

And all things, whatsoever ye shall ask in prayer, believing, ye shall receive.

I have to write and give God all the honor and the glory for answered prayers! A few days ago I stood on a mountain top overlooking God's beautiful creation. I watched my friends share their wedding vows in an outdoor ceremony on a day that the weathermen predicted to be filled with severe weather. We prayed for good weather, claimed it and left it in God's hands, with the promise to give Him all the glory! It was an overcast windy day, with not a drop of rain! As the bride and groom readied to leave, I took her face in my hands and said, "Look up, God answers prayers!" How amazing is the God that I serve that He cared about my friends that day so much that He changed the weather! He took away the storms and replaced them with gentle breezes!

Thank You God for showing up and showing out, You prove to me over and over that You listen to our prayers. I stand amazed in Your presence more each day!

Heritage

Psalm 127:3

Lo, children are an heritage of the LORD: and the fruit of the womb is his reward.

My mom loved quotes and my daughter loves them too. She has a lot of quotes she has written in a book. This morning I was looking through her book of quotes when some old letters fell out. They were letters I had written to her during some challenging times. Since I had written them to begin with I reread them. They brought me to tears as I remembered the struggles she was going through during that time. I found myself reading words that I had forgotten writing, words to encourage her and praise her. Words to remind her where to look as she forged onward to her goals. One of those letters was during a time when she was trying to decide about college, it was breaking my heart to think of her moving away to school. I poured my heart out to her about it all in one of those letters. I had written that I was praying for God to give her a clear answer and me peace to understand it. I know from experience how hard it is for us to let our children grow up, it seemed like I was all alone in having to do this. I can look back now and see God's hand leading both of us as she made the decisions that she made. I actually won out on this one as she stayed home and went to college, but God knew all along His plans for her. We can both see that God has her right where He wants her now. I am so thankful for my beautiful daughter and her faith in our Lord. Truly, children are a heritage from the Lord!

Lord, thank You so much for my beautiful daughter, thank You for guiding us as we raised her, but most of all thank You that she has a heart for You.

SHINE

Matthew 5:16

In the same way, let your light shine before others, so that they may see your good works and give glory to your Father who is in heaven.

"This little light of mine, I'm gonna let it shine". Do you remember this sweet little song from your childhood? We sang it out loud and clear with huge smiles on our faces during children's choir. Have we grown up and forgotten that little song? Even further, have we forgotten to let our light shine for Jesus? We find it easy to talk about other things in our lives that are important. We don't hesitate to tell others how great our kids and grandkids are. We should be even more zealous about sharing how great our God is! Don't hide the greatness of God "under a bushel." Let your light shine for Him.

Father, let us be a beacon in this dark world, pointing others to You.

Relief

Psalm 23:4

Yea, though I walk through the valley of the shadow of death, I will fear no evil: for thou art with me; thy rod and thy staff they comfort me.

Over the years I have dealt with some anxiety issues. When I am sick and start to feel really bad, I tend to panic. Of course, that just makes things worse. If you've ever dealt with anxiety, you know how quickly you can see yourself in peril. Waking up startled, shaky, sweating, with your heart beating too fast is scary. Thinking the worst is going to happen is even scarier. And yes, I've even felt like I was going to die. During these episodes I often recite the 23rd Psalm until my anxiety leaves. I can feel myself calming down as I say the words, taking each of them to heart. Allowing myself to relax and breathe normally, I begin to feel better. Anytime that my fears take control I quote these verses. God gave us these sweet words to help us on our way. He knew there would be times when we needed assurance that He would be with us.

Thank You God, for giving me words of hope even when my mind is being over-active and I'm just afraid. Thank You for Your words of encouragement, that no matter what we face, You will carry us through.

IMMERSED

Deuteronomy 11:18

Therefore shall ye lay up these my words in your heart and in your soul, and bind them for a sign upon your hand, that they may be as frontlets between your eyes.

Now more than ever, I realize how powerful God's word is! It's been a pure joy for me to search out and study God's beautiful scriptures in order to share them with you. God has shown me His word in a new way and how much He wants us to know His word, inside and out. He desires us to hold it in our hearts and to be ready always to share it for His glory! My prayer is that you will hide HIS words in your hearts and souls and use them to share HIS love!

Father, when I began this journey I knew You had something wonderful to share with me, I'm humbled that You allowed me the opportunity to learn more about You and Your promises. I pray that as I continue to learn from You that You will continue to give me opportunities to share Your love.

About the Author

Marti Owens is introducing *My Shelter* as her first book of devotions. She has always had a love for writing and is excited to have *My Shelter* published. Marti lives in a rural town in Alabama with her husband, Yorkie, Poodle and cat and her family close by. She enjoys reading.

WORK CITED

"PRAISE" 1, Thorndike + Barnhart Junior Dictionary, Copyright 1962

CPSIA information can be obtained at www.ICGtesting.com
Printed in the USA
LVOW04s0630250815

451342LV00003B/4/P